MznLnx

Missing Links Exam Preps

Exam Prep for

Algebra and Trigonometry With Analytic Geometry

Swokowski, Cole, 11th Edition

The MznLnx Exam Prep is your link from the texbook and lecture to your exams.
The MznLnx Exam Preps are unauthorized and comprehensive reviews of your textbooks.

All material provided by MznLnx and Rico Publications (c) 2010
Textbook publishers and textbook authors do not particpate in or contribute to these reviews.

MznLnx

Rico Publications

Exam Prep for Algebra and Trigonometry With Analytic Geometry
11th Edition
Swokowski, Cole

Publisher: Raymond Houge
Assistant Editor: Michael Rouger
Text and Cover Designer: Lisa Buckner
Marketing Manager: Sara Swagger
Project Manager, Editorial Production: Jerry Emerson
Art Director: Vernon Lowerui

Product Manager: Dave Mason
Editorial Assitant: Rachel Guzmanji
Pedagogy: Debra Long
Cover Image: Jim Reed/Getty Images
Text and Cover Printer: City Printing, Inc.
Compositor: Media Mix, Inc.

(c) 2010 Rico Publications
ALL RIGHTS RESERVED. No part of this work covered by the copyright may be reproduced or used in any form or by an means--graphic, electronic, or mechanical, including photocopying, recording, taping, Web distribution, information storage, and retrieval systems, or in any other manner--without the written permission of the publisher.

Printed in the United States
ISBN:

For more information about our products, contact us at:
Dave.Mason@RicoPublications.com

For permission to use material from this text or product, submit a request online to:
Dave.Mason@RicoPublications.com

Contents

CHAPTER 1
Fundamental Concepts of Algebra — 1

CHAPTER 2
Equations and Inequalities — 14

CHAPTER 3
Functions and Graphs — 25

CHAPTER 4
Polynomial and Rational Functions — 38

CHAPTER 5
Inverse, Exponential, and Logarithmic Functions — 45

CHAPTER 6
The Trigonometric Functions — 54

CHAPTER 7
Analytic Trigonometry — 68

CHAPTER 8
Applications of Trigonometry — 74

CHAPTER 9
Systems of Equations and Inequalities — 83

CHAPTER 10
Sequences, Series, and Probability — 95

CHAPTER 11
Topics from Analytic Geometry — 105

ANSWER KEY — 116

TO THE STUDENT

COMPREHENSIVE

The *MznLnx* Exam Prep series is designed to help you pass your exams. Editors at MznLnx review your textbooks and then prepare these practice exams to help you master the textbook material. Unlike study guides, workbooks, and practice tests provided by the texbook publisher and textbook authors, *MznLnx* gives you **all** of the material in each chapter in exam form, not just samples, so you can be sure to nail your exam.

MECHANICAL

The MznLnx Exam Prep series creates exams that will help you learn the subject matter as well as test you on your understanding. Each question is designed to help you master the concept. Just working through the exams, you gain an understanding of the subject--its a simple mechanical process that produces success.

INTEGRATED STUDY GUIDE AND REVIEW

MznLnx is not just a set of exams designed to test you, its also a comprehensive review of the subject content. Each exam question is also a review of the concept, making sure that you will get the answer correct without having to go to other sources of material. You learn as you go! Its the easiest way to pass an exam.

HUMOR

Studying can be tedious and dry. MznLnx's instructional design includes moderate humor within the exam questions on occassion, to break the tedium and revitalize the brain

Chapter 1. Fundamental Concepts of Algebra   1

1. In mathematics, a _____ of an integer n is an integer which evenly divides n without leaving a remainder.

For example, 7 is a _____ of 42 because 42/7 = 6. We also say 42 is divisible by 7 or 42 is a multiple of 7 or 7 divides 42 or 7 is a factor of 42 and we usually write 7 | 42.

- a. Divisor
- b. 2-3 heap
- c. 1-center problem
- d. 120-cell

2. In mathematics, the _____ states that every non-constant single-variable polynomial with complex coefficients has at least one complex root. Equivalently, the field of complex numbers is algebraically closed.

Sometimes, this theorem is stated as: every non-zero single-variable polynomial, with complex coefficients, has exactly as many complex roots as its degree, if each root is counted up to its multiplicity.

- a. Closure with a twist
- b. Distributive
- c. Near-semiring
- d. Fundamental theorem of algebra

3. The _____ are the set of numbers consisting of the natural numbers including 0 and their negatives. They are numbers that can be written without a fractional or decimal component, and fall within the set {... −2, −1, 0, 1, 2, ...}.

- a. Integers
- b. A posteriori
- c. A chemical equation
- d. A Mathematical Theory of Communication

4. In mathematics, a _____ can mean either an element of the set {1, 2, 3, ...} or an element of the set {0, 1, 2, 3, ...}. The latter is especially preferred in mathematical logic, set theory, and computer science.

_____s have two main purposes: they can be used for counting, and they can be used for ordering.

- a. Suslin cardinal
- b. Natural number
- c. Cardinal numbers
- d. Strong partition cardinal

5. In mathematics, a _____ is a natural number which has exactly two distinct natural number divisors: 1 and itself. An infinitude of _____s exists, as demonstrated by Euclid around 300 BC. The first twenty-five _____s are:

2, 3, 5, 7, 11, 13, 17, 19, 23, 29, 31, 37, 41, 43, 47, 53, 59, 61, 67, 71, 73, 79, 83, 89, 97.

- a. Highly composite number
- b. Perrin number
- c. Prime number
- d. Pronic number

6. In mathematics, a _____ is a number which can be expressed as a ratio of two integers. Non-integer _____s are usually written as the vulgar fraction $\frac{a}{b}$, where b is not zero. a is called the numerator, and b the denominator.

- a. Minkowski distance
- b. Tally marks
- c. Pre-algebra
- d. Rational number

Chapter 1. Fundamental Concepts of Algebra

7. In mathematics, the _____s may be described informally in several different ways. The _____s include both rational numbers, such as 42 and −23/129, and irrational numbers, such as pi and the square root of two; or, a _____ can be given by an infinite decimal representation, such as 2.4871773339...., where the digits continue in some way; or, the _____s may be thought of as points on an infinitely long number line.

These descriptions of the _____s, while intuitively accessible, are not sufficiently rigorous for the purposes of pure mathematics.

    a. Pre-algebra   b. Minkowski distance
    c. Real number   d. Tally marks

8. In vascular plants, the _____ is the organ of a plant body that typically lies below the surface of the soil. This is not always the case, however, since a _____ can also be aerial (that is, growing above the ground) or aerating (that is, growing up above the ground or especially above water.) Furthermore, a stem normally occurring below ground is not exceptional either

    a. 1-center problem   b. 120-cell
    c. Root   d. 2-3 heap

9. In mathematics, a _____ can mean either an element of the set {1, 2, 3, ...} (i.e the positive integers) or an element of the set {0, 1, 2, 3, ...} (i.e. the non-negative integers).

    a. Whole number   b. Bounded
    c. FISH   d. Degrees of freedom

10. In mathematics, a _____ is a statement that can be proved on the basis of explicitly stated or previously agreed assumptions.

    a. Boolean function   b. Logical value
    c. Theorem   d. Disjunction introduction

11. In mathematics, a _____ of a number x is a number r such that r^2 = x, or, in other words, a number r whose square is x. Every non-negative real number x has a unique non-negative _____, called the principal _____, which is denoted with a radical symbol as $\sqrt{x}$, or, using exponent notation, as $x^{1/2}$. For example, the principal _____ of 9 is 3, denoted $\sqrt{9}$ = 3, because 3^2 = 3 × 3 = 9.

    a. Double exponential   b. Square root
    c. Multiplicative inverse   d. Hyperbolic functions

12. In mathematics, an arithmetic progression or _____ is a sequence of numbers such that the difference of any two successive members of the sequence is a constant. For instance, the sequence 3, 5, 7, 9, 11, 13... is an arithmetic progression with common difference 2.

    a. Edgeworth series   b. Alternating series test
    c. Eisenstein series   d. Arithmetic sequence

13. In mathematics, the _____s are an extension of the real numbers obtained by adjoining an imaginary unit, denoted i, which satisfies:

$i^2 = -1.$

Every _____ can be written in the form a + bi, where a and b are real numbers called the real part and the imaginary part of the _____, respectively.

_____s are a field, and thus have addition, subtraction, multiplication, and division operations. These operations extend the corresponding operations on real numbers, although with a number of additional elegant and useful properties, e.g., negative real numbers can be obtained by squaring _____s.

- a. 120-cell
- b. Real part
- c. 1-center problem
- d. Complex number

14. In mathematics the _____ of a set which is equipped with the operation of addition is an element which, when added to any element x in the set, yields x. One of the most familiar additive identities is the number 0 from elementary mathematics, but additive identities occur in other mathematical structures where addition is defined, such as in groups and rings.

- The _____ familiar from elementary mathematics is zero, denoted 0. For example,

5 + 0 = 5 = 0 + 5.

- In the natural numbers N and all of its supersets, the _____ is 0. Thus for any one of these numbers n,

n + 0 = n = 0 + n.

Let N be a set which is closed under the operation of addition, denoted +. An _____ for N is any element e such that for any element n in N,

e + n = n = n + e.

- a. Additive identity
- b. Algebraically independent
- c. Unit ring
- d. Unique factorization domain

15. In mathematics, the _____ of a number n is the number that, when added to n, yields zero. The _____ of n is denoted −n. For example, 7 is −7, because 7 + (−7) = 0, and the _____ of −0.3 is 0.3, because −0.3 + 0.3 = 0.
- a. Arity
- b. Algebraic structure
- c. Additive inverse
- d. Associativity

16. In mathematics, _____ is a property that a binary operation can have. It means that, within an expression containing two or more of the same associative operators in a row, the order that the operations are performed does not matter as long as the sequence of the operands is not changed. That is, rearranging the parentheses in such an expression will not change its value.

a. Algebraically closed
c. Associativity
b. Unital
d. Idempotence

17. In mathematics, and in particular in abstract algebra, distributivity is a property of binary operations that generalises the _____ law from elementary algebra.
   a. Closure with a twist
   b. Distributive
   c. General linear group
   d. Permutation

18. In mathematics, the term _____ has several different important meanings:

   - An _____ is an equality that remains true regardless of the values of any variables that appear within it, to distinguish it from an equality which is true under more particular conditions. For this, the 'triple bar' symbol ≡ is sometimes used.
   - In algebra, an _____ or _____ element of a set S with a binary operation Â· is an element e that, when combined with any element x of S, produces that same x. That is, eÂ·x = xÂ·e = x for all x in S.
     - The _____ function from a set S to itself, often denoted id or id_S, s the function such that i = x for all x in S. This function serves as the _____ element in the set of all functions from S to itself with respect to function composition.
     - In linear algebra, the _____ matrix of size n is the n-by-n square matrix with ones on the main diagonal and zeros elsewhere. This matrix serves as the _____ with respect to matrix multiplication.

A common example of the first meaning is the trigonometric _____

$$\sin^2 \theta + \cos^2 \theta = 1$$

which is true for all real values of θ, as opposed to

$$\cos \theta = 1,$$

which is true only for some values of θ, not all. For example, the latter equation is true when $\theta = 0$, false when $\theta = 2$

The concepts of 'additive _____' and 'multiplicative _____' are central to the Peano axioms. The number 0 is the 'additive _____' for integers, real numbers, and complex numbers. For the real numbers, for all $a \in \mathbb{R}$,

$$0 + a = a,$$

$$a + 0 = a,$$ and

$$0 + 0 = 0.$$

Similarly, The number 1 is the 'multiplicative _____' for integers, real numbers, and complex numbers.

    a. Intersection
    b. Action
    c. ARIA
    d. Identity

19. _____ is the mathematical operation of scaling one number by another. It is one of the four basic operations in elementary arithmetic.

_____ is defined for whole numbers in terms of repeated addition; for example, 4 multiplied by 3 can be calculated by adding 3 copies of 4 together:

$$4 + 4 + 4 = 12.$$

_____ of rational numbers and real numbers is defined by systematic generalization of this basic idea.

    a. The number 0 is even.
    b. Highest common factor
    c. Multiplication
    d. Least common multiple

20. In mathematics, a _____ for a number x, denoted by $1/x$ or x^{-1}, is a number which when multiplied by x yields the multiplicative identity, 1. The _____ of x is also called the reciprocal of x. The _____ of a fraction p/q is q/p.

    a. Golden function
    b. Hyperbolic function
    c. Double exponential
    d. Multiplicative inverse

21. In mathematics, the multiplicative inverse of a number x, denoted 1/x or x^{-1}, is the number which, when multiplied by x, yields 1. The multiplicative inverse of x is also called the _____ of x.

    a. 120-cell
    b. Reciprocal
    c. 2-3 heap
    d. 1-center problem

22. In mathematics, the _____ of a real number is its numerical value without regard to its sign. So, for example, 3 is the _____ of both 3 and −3.

The _____ of a number a is denoted by $|a|$.

Generalizations of the _____ for real numbers occur in a wide variety of mathematical settings.

    a. A chemical equation
    b. Absolute value
    c. A Mathematical Theory of Communication
    d. Area hyperbolic functions

23. In mathematics and in the sciences, a _____ (plural: _____e, formulæ or _____s) is a concise way of expressing information symbolically (as in a mathematical or chemical _____), or a general relationship between quantities. One of many famous _____e is Albert Einstein's E = mc² (see special relativity

In mathematics, a _____ is a key to solve an equation with variables. For example, the problem of determining the volume of a sphere is one that requires a significant amount of integral calculus to solve.

Chapter 1. Fundamental Concepts of Algebra

a. 2-3 heap
b. 120-cell
c. 1-center problem
d. Formula

24. _____ is a branch of mathematics which focuses on the study of matrices. Initially a sub-branch of linear algebra, it has grown to cover subjects related to graph theory, algebra, combinatorics, and statistics as well.

The term matrix was first coined in 1848 by J.J. Sylvester as a name of an array of numbers.

a. Semi-simple operators
b. Matrix theory
c. Segre classification
d. Pairing

25. In mathematics, a _____ is the end result of a division problem. It can also be expressed as the number of times the divisor divides into the dividend.

a. Notation
b. Limiting
c. Marginal cost
d. Quotient

26. In mathematics, the _____ of a Euclidean space is a special point, usually denoted by the letter O, used as a fixed point of reference for the geometry of the surrounding space. In a Cartesian coordinate system, the _____ is the point where the axes of the system intersect. In Euclidean geometry, the _____ may be chosen freely as any convenient point of reference.

a. Autonomous system
b. Interval
c. OMAC
d. Origin

27. In mathematics, an inequality is a statement about the relative size or order of two objects. For example 14 > 10, or 14 is _____ 10. The notation a > b means that a is _____ b and 'a' would be to the right of 'b' on a number line.

a. Cauchy-Schwarz inequality
b. Minkowski inequality
c. Greater than
d. FKG inequality

28. In mathematics, an _____ is a statement about the relative size or order of two objects, or about whether they are the same or not

- The notation a < b means that a is less than b.
- The notation a > b means that a is greater than b.
- The notation a ≠ b means that a is not equal to b, but does not say that one is bigger than the other or even that they can be compared in size.

In all these cases, a is not equal to b, hence, '_____'.

These relations are known as strict _____

- The notation a ≤ b means that a is less than or equal to b;
- The notation a ≥ b means that a is greater than or equal to b;

Chapter 1. Fundamental Concepts of Algebra

An additional use of the notation is to show that one quantity is much greater than another, normally by several orders of magnitude.

- The notation a << b means that a is much less than b.
- The notation a >> b means that a is much greater than b.

If the sense of the _____ is the same for all values of the variables for which its members are defined, then the _____ is called an 'absolute' or 'unconditional' _____. If the sense of an _____ holds only for certain values of the variables involved, but is reversed or destroyed for other values of the variables, it is called a conditional _____.

An _____ may appear unsolvable because it only states whether a number is larger or smaller than another number; but it is possible to apply the same operations for equalities to inequalities. For example, to find x for the _____ 10x > 23 one would divide 23 by 10.

a. A Mathematical Theory of Communication
b. A chemical equation
c. Inequality
d. A posteriori

29. In trigonometry, the _____ is a statement about a general triangle which relates the lengths of its sides to the cosine of one of its angles. Using notation as in Fig. 1, the _____ states that

$$c^2 = a^2 + b^2 - 2ab\cos(\gamma),$$

or, equivalently:

$$b^2 = c^2 + a^2 - 2ca\cos(\beta),$$
$$a^2 = b^2 + c^2 - 2bc\cos(\alpha),$$
$$\cos(\gamma) = \frac{a^2 + b^2 - c^2}{2ab}.$$

Note that c is the side opposite of angle γ, and that a and b are the two sides enclosing γ.

a. Law of tangents
b. Trigonometric functions
c. Law of cosines
d. Trigonometric

30. In mathematical writing, the adjective _____ is used to modify technical terms which have multiple meanings. It indicates that the exclusive meaning of the term is to be understood. (More formally, one could say that this is the meaning which implies the other meanings.)

a. Well-behaved
b. Jargon
c. Percentage points
d. Strict

31. In mathematics and computer science, _____ (also base-16, hexa or base, of 16. It uses sixteen distinct symbols, most often the symbols 0-9 to represent values zero to nine, and A, B, C, D, E, F (or a through f) to represent values ten to fifteen.

Its primary use is as a human friendly representation of binary coded values, so it is often used in digital electronics and computer engineering.

a. Hexadecimal
b. Radix
c. Factoradic
d. Tetradecimal

32. Exponentiation is a mathematical operation, written a^n, involving two numbers, the base a and the _____ n. When n is a positive integer, exponentiation corresponds to repeated multiplication:

$$a^n = \underbrace{a \times \cdots \times a}_{n},$$

just as multiplication by a positive integer corresponds to repeated addition:

$$a \times n = \underbrace{a + \cdots + a}_{n}.$$

The _____ is usually shown as a superscript to the right of the base. The exponentiation a^n can be read as: a raised to the n-th power, a raised to the power [of] n or possibly a raised to the _____ [of] n, or more briefly: a to the n-th power or a to the power [of] n, or even more briefly: a to the n.

a. Exponential tree
b. Exponential sum
c. Exponentiating by squaring
d. Exponent

33. Scientific notation, also sometimes known as standard form or as _____, is a way of writing numbers that accommodates values too large or small to be conveniently written in standard decimal notation. Scientific notation has a number of useful properties and is often favored by scientists, mathematicians and engineers, who work with such numbers.

In scientific notation, numbers are written in the form:

$$a \times 10^b$$

a. A posteriori
b. A Mathematical Theory of Communication
c. A chemical equation
d. Exponential notation

34. In mathematics, the _____s are analogs of the ordinary trigonometric functions. The basic _____s are the hyperbolic sine 'sinh', and the hyperbolic cosine 'cosh', from which are derived the hyperbolic tangent 'tanh', etc., in analogy to the derived trigonometric functions. The inverse _____ are the area hyperbolic sine 'arsinh' (also called 'asinh', or sometimes by the misnomer of 'arcsinh') and so on.

Chapter 1. Fundamental Concepts of Algebra

a. Heaviside step function
b. Rectangular function
c. Hyperbolic function
d. Square root

35. In geometry, a _____ is a part of a line that is bounded by two distinct end points, and contains every point on the line between its end points. Examples of _____s include the sides of a triangle or square. More generally, when the end points are both vertices of a polygon, the _____ is either an edge if they are adjacent vertices, or otherwise a diagonal.
    a. Golden angle
    b. Transversal line
    c. Cuboid
    d. Line segment

36. A _____ is a device for performing mathematical calculations, distinguished from a computer by having a limited problem solving ability and an interface optimized for interactive calculation rather than programming. _____s can be hardware or software, and mechanical or electronic, and are often built into devices such as PDAs or mobile phones.

    Modern electronic _____s are generally small, digital, and usually inexpensive.

    a. 120-cell
    b. 2-3 heap
    c. Calculator
    d. 1-center problem

37. In mathematics, the _____ is a term used to describe the number of times one must apply a given operation to an integer before reaching a fixed point.

    Usually, this refers to the additive or multiplicative persistence of an integer, which is how often one has to replace the number by the sum or product of its digits until one reaches a single digit. Because the numbers are broken down into their digits, the additive or multiplicative persistence depends on the radix.

    a. Coprime
    b. Linear congruence theorem
    c. Lychrel number
    d. Persistence of a number

38. The _____ of a number are those digits that carry meaning contributing to its precision. This includes all digits except:

    - leading and trailing zeros where they serve merely as placeholders to indicate the scale of the number.
    - spurious digits introduced, for example, by calculations carried out to greater accuracy than that of the original data, or measurements reported to a greater precision than the equipment supports.

    The concept of _____ is often used in connection with rounding. Rounding to n _____ is a more general-purpose technique than rounding to n decimal places, since it handles numbers of different scales in a uniform way. A practical calculation that uses any irrational number necessitates rounding the number, and hence the answer, to a finite number of _____.

    a. Tetration
    b. Rounding
    c. Shabakh
    d. Significant figures

39. In mathematics, a _____ is a constant multiplicative factor of a certain object. For example, in the expression $9x^2$, the _____ of x^2 is 9.

The object can be such things as a variable, a vector, a function, etc.

a. Fibonacci polynomials
b. Coefficient
c. Stability radius
d. Multivariate division algorithm

40. In simple terms, two events are _____ if they cannot occur at the same time.

In logic, two _____ propositions are propositions that logically cannot both be true. To say that more than two propositions are _____ may, depending on context mean that no two of them can both be true, or only that they cannot all be true.

a. Philosophy
b. Determinism
c. Philosophy of mathematics
d. Mutually exclusive

41. In probability theory, an _____ is a set of outcomes to which a probability is assigned. Typically, when the sample space is finite, any subset of the sample space is an _____. However, this approach does not work well in cases where the sample space is infinite, most notably when the outcome is a real number.

a. Equaliser
b. Audio compression
c. Information set
d. Event

42. A _____ of a number is a number a such that $a^3 = x$.

a. Golden function
b. Cube root
c. Square root
d. Hyperbolic functions

43. In mathematics, an algebraic group G contains a unique maximal normal solvable subgroup; and this subgroup is closed. Its identity component is called the _____ of G.

a. Radical
b. Block size
c. Composite
d. Barycentric coordinates

44. In mathematics, an _____ or member of a set is any one of the distinct objects that make up that set.

Writing A = {1,2,3,4}, means that the _____s of the set A are the numbers 1, 2, 3 and 4. Groups of _____s of A, for example {1,2}, are subsets of A.

a. Universal code
b. Ideal
c. Order
d. Element

45. In mathematics, especially in set theory, a set A is a _____ of a set B if A is 'contained' inside B. Notice that A and B may coincide. The relationship of one set being a _____ of another is called inclusion.

a. Subset
b. Horizontal line test
c. Set of all sets
d. Cartesian product

46. In mathematics, a _____ is a rectangular table of elements, which may be numbers or, more generally, any abstract quantities that can be added and multiplied. Matrices are used to describe linear equations, keep track of the coefficients of linear transformations and to record data that depend on multiple parameters. Matrices are described by the field of _____ theory.

   a. Double counting   b. Coherent
   c. Compression   d. Matrix

47. In abstract algebra, a field extension L /K is called _____ if every element of L is _____ over K. Field extensions which are not _____.

For example, the field extension R/Q, that is the field of real numbers as an extension of the field of rational numbers, is transcendental, while the field extensions C/R and Q

   a. Ideal   b. Identity
   c. Echo   d. Algebraic

48. In elementary algebra, a _____ is a polynomial with two terms: the sum of two monomials. It is the simplest kind of polynomial except for a monomial.

The _____ $a^2 - b^2$ can be factored as the product of two other _____ s:

   $a^2 - b^2$.

The product of a pair of linear _____ s a x + b and c x + d is:

   2 +x + bd.

A _____ raised to the nth power, represented as

   n

can be expanded by means of the _____ theorem or, equivalently, using Pascal's triangle.

   a. Cylindrical algebraic decomposition   b. Real structure
   c. Rational root theorem   d. Binomial

49. In mathematics, especially in the area of abstract algebra known as ring theory, a _____ is a ring with 0 ≠ 1 such that ab = 0 implies that either a = 0 or b = 0. That is, it is a nontrivial ring without left or right zero divisors. A commutative _____ is called an integral _____.

   a. Left primitive ring   b. Modular representation theory
   c. Simple ring   d. Domain

50. In the study of metric spaces in mathematics, there are various notions of two metrics on the same underlying space being 'the same', or _____.

Chapter 1. Fundamental Concepts of Algebra

In the following, M will denote a non-empty set and d_1 and d_2 will denote two metrics on M.

The two metrics d_1 and d_2 are said to be topologically _____ if they generate the same topology on M.

a. Equivalent
b. A chemical equation
c. A Mathematical Theory of Communication
d. A posteriori

51. In mathematics, the word _____ means two different things in the context of polynomials:

- The first meaning is a product of powers of variables, or formally any value obtained from 1 by finitely many multiplications by a variable. If only a single variable x is considered this means that any _____ is either 1 or a power x^n of x, with n a positive integer. If several variables are considered, say, x, y, z, then each can be given an exponent, so that any _____ is of the form $x^a y^b z^c$ with a,b,c nonnegative integers.
- The second meaning of _____ includes _____s in the first sense, but also allows multiplication by any constant, so that $-7x^5$ and $4yz^{13}$ are also considered to be _____s.

With either definition, the set of _____s is a subset of all polynomials that is closed under multiplication.

a. Diagonal form
b. Homogeneous polynomial
c. Power sum symmetric polynomial
d. Monomial

52. In mathematics, a _____ is an expression constructed from variables and constants, using the operations of addition, subtraction, multiplication, and constant non-negative whole number exponents. For example, $x^2 - 4x + 7$ is a _____, but $x^2 - 4/x + 7x^{3/2}$ is not, because its second term involves division by the variable x and also because its third term contains an exponent that is not a whole number.

_____s are one of the most important concepts in algebra and throughout mathematics and science.

a. Group extension
b. Semifield
c. Coimage
d. Polynomial

53. In elementary algebra, a _____ is a polynomial consisting of three terms; in other words, a _____ is the sum of three monomials. It can be factored using simple steps

In linguistics, a _____ is a fixed expression which is made from three words; e.g. 'lights, camera, action', 'signed, sealed, delivered'.

a. Recurrence relation
b. Relation algebra
c. Trinomial
d. Symmetric difference

54. The framework of quantum mechanics requires a careful definition of _____, and a thorough discussion of its practical and philosophical implications.

_____ is viewed in different ways in the many interpretations of quantum mechanics; however, despite the considerable philosophical differences, they almost universally agree on the practical question of what results from a routine quantum-physics laboratory _____. To describe this, a simple framework to use is the Copenhagen interpretation, and it will be implicitly used in this section; the utility of this approach has been verified countless times, and all other interpretations are necessarily constructed so as to give the same quantitative predictions as this in almost every case.

a. 1-center problem
b. Dynamic range
c. Measurement
d. Fundamental units

55. In mathematics, the adjective _____ means that an object cannot be expressed as a product of at least two non-trivial factors in a given set.

For any field F, the ring of polynomials with coefficients in F is denoted by F[x].

a. Integer-valued polynomial
b. Ehrhart polynomial
c. Euler-Worpitzky-Chen polynomials
d. Irreducible

56. _____ is an algebraic technique used to solve quadratic equations, in analytic geometry for determining the shapes of graphs, and in calculus for computing integrals. The essential objective is to reduce a quadratic polynomial in a variable in an equation or expression to a squared polynomial of linear order. This can reduce an equation or integral to one that is more easily solved or evaluated.

a. Monomial basis
b. Relation algebra
c. Permanent of a matrix
d. Completing the square

57. In mathematics, the _____ or least common denominator is the least common multiple of the denominators of a set of vulgar fractions. It is the smallest positive integer that is a multiple of the denominators. For instance, the _____ of

$$\left\{\frac{5}{12}, \frac{11}{18}\right\}$$

is 36 because the least common multiple of 12 and 18 is 36.

a. The number 0 is even.
b. Subtrahend
c. Highest common factor
d. Lowest common denominator

Chapter 2. Equations and Inequalities

1. In the study of metric spaces in mathematics, there are various notions of two metrics on the same underlying space being 'the same', or _____.

   In the following, M will denote a non-empty set and d_1 and d_2 will denote two metrics on M.

   The two metrics d_1 and d_2 are said to be topologically _____ if they generate the same topology on M.

   a. A posteriori
   b. Equivalent
   c. A chemical equation
   d. A Mathematical Theory of Communication

2. In vascular plants, the _____ is the organ of a plant body that typically lies below the surface of the soil. This is not always the case, however, since a _____ can also be aerial (that is, growing above the ground) or aerating (that is, growing up above the ground or especially above water.) Furthermore, a stem normally occurring below ground is not exceptional either
   a. 120-cell
   b. 2-3 heap
   c. 1-center problem
   d. Root

3. In abstract algebra, a field extension L /K is called _____ if every element of L is _____ over K. Field extensions which are not _____.

   For example, the field extension R/Q, that is the field of real numbers as an extension of the field of rational numbers, is transcendental, while the field extensions C/R and Q

   a. Algebraic
   b. Echo
   c. Identity
   d. Ideal

4. In mathematics, an _____ over a given field is an equation of the form

   P = Q

   where P and Q are polynomials over that field. For example

   $$y^4 + \frac{xy}{2} = \frac{x^3}{3} - xy^2 + y^2 - \frac{1}{7}$$

   is an _____ over the rationals.

   Note that an _____ over the rationals can always be converted to an equivalent one in which the coefficients are integers.

   a. Irreducible
   b. Euler-Worpitzky-Chen polynomials
   c. Ehrhart polynomial
   d. Algebraic equation

Chapter 2. Equations and Inequalities

5. In mathematics, the term _____ has several different important meanings:

   - An _____ is an equality that remains true regardless of the values of any variables that appear within it, to distinguish it from an equality which is true under more particular conditions. For this, the 'triple bar' symbol ≡ is sometimes used.
   - In algebra, an _____ or _____ element of a set S with a binary operation Â· is an element e that, when combined with any element x of S, produces that same x. That is, eÂ·x = xÂ·e = x for all x in S.
     - The _____ function from a set S to itself, often denoted id or id_S, s the function such that i = x for all x in S. This function serves as the _____ element in the set of all functions from S to itself with respect to function composition.
     - In linear algebra, the _____ matrix of size n is the n-by-n square matrix with ones on the main diagonal and zeros elsewhere. This matrix serves as the _____ with respect to matrix multiplication.

A common example of the first meaning is the trigonometric _____

$$\sin^2 \theta + \cos^2 \theta = 1$$

which is true for all real values of θ, as opposed to

$$\cos \theta = 1,$$

which is true only for some values of θ, not all. For example, the latter equation is true when $\theta = 0$, false when $\theta = 2$

The concepts of 'additive _____' and 'multiplicative _____' are central to the Peano axioms. The number 0 is the 'additive _____' for integers, real numbers, and complex numbers. For the real numbers, for all $a \in \mathbb{R}$,

$$0 + a = a,$$

$$a + 0 = a, \text{ and}$$

$$0 + 0 = 0.$$

Similarly, The number 1 is the 'multiplicative _____' for integers, real numbers, and complex numbers.

a. Action
c. ARIA
b. Identity
d. Intersection

6. A _____ is an algebraic equation in which each term is either a constant or the product of a constant and a single variable. _____s can have one, two, three or more variables.

_____s occur with great regularity in applied mathematics.

a. Linear equation
c. Difference of two squares
b. Quartic equation
d. Quadratic equation

7. In linear algebra a matrix is in _____ if

- All nonzero rows are above any rows of all zeroes, and
- The leading coefficient of a row is always strictly to the right of the leading coefficient of the row above it.

This is the definition used in this article, but some texts add a third condition:

- The leading coefficient of each nonzero row is one.

A matrix is in reduced _____ if it satisfies the above three conditions, and if, in addition

- Every leading coefficient is the only nonzero entry in its column.

The first non-zero entry in each row is called a pivot.

This matrix is in reduced _____:

$$\begin{bmatrix} 0 & 1 & 4 & 0 & 0 \\ 0 & 0 & 0 & 1 & 0 \\ 0 & 0 & 0 & 0 & 1 \\ 0 & 0 & 0 & 0 & 0 \end{bmatrix}.$$

The following matrix is also in _____, but not in reduced row form:

$$\begin{bmatrix} 1 & 1 & 1 & 1 \\ 0 & 9 & 0 & 2 \\ 0 & 0 & 0 & 3 \end{bmatrix}.$$

However, this matrix is not in _____, as the leading coefficient of row 3 is not strictly to the right of the leading coefficient of row 2.

$$\begin{bmatrix} 1 & 2 & 3 & 4 \\ 0 & 3 & 7 & 2 \\ 0 & 2 & 0 & 0 \end{bmatrix}$$

Every non-zero matrix can be reduced to an infinite number of echelon forms via elementary matrix transformations.

Chapter 2. Equations and Inequalities

a. Gaussian elimination
c. Reduced row echelon form
b. Portable, Extensible Toolkit for Scientific Computation
d. Row echelon form

8. In mathematics, a _____ is a rectangular table of elements, which may be numbers or, more generally, any abstract quantities that can be added and multiplied. Matrices are used to describe linear equations, keep track of the coefficients of linear transformations and to record data that depend on multiple parameters. Matrices are described by the field of _____ theory.

a. Compression
c. Matrix
b. Coherent
d. Double counting

9. In mathematics and in the sciences, a _____ (plural: _____e, formulæ or _____s) is a concise way of expressing information symbolically (as in a mathematical or chemical _____), or a general relationship between quantities. One of many famous _____e is Albert Einstein's $E = mc^2$ (see special relativity

In mathematics, a _____ is a key to solve an equation with variables. For example, the problem of determining the volume of a sphere is one that requires a significant amount of integral calculus to solve.

a. 1-center problem
c. 2-3 heap
b. Formula
d. 120-cell

10. _____ is a fee, paid on borrowed capital. Assets lent include money, shares, consumer goods through hire purchase, major assets such as aircraft, and even entire factories in finance lease arrangements. The _____ is calculated upon the value of the assets in the same manner as upon money.

a. Interest expense
c. Interest sensitivity gap
b. A Mathematical Theory of Communication
d. Interest

11. In abstract algebra, a module S over a ring R is called _____ or irreducible if it is not the zero module 0 and if its only submodules are 0 and S. Understanding the _____ modules over a ring is usually helpful because these modules form the 'building blocks' of all other modules in a certain sense.

Abelian groups are the same as Z-modules.

a. Harmonic series
c. Simple
b. Basis
d. Derivation

12. In mathematics and computer science, _____ (also base-16, hexa or base, of 16. It uses sixteen distinct symbols, most often the symbols 0-9 to represent values zero to nine, and A, B, C, D, E, F (or a through f) to represent values ten to fifteen.

Its primary use is as a human friendly representation of binary coded values, so it is often used in digital electronics and computer engineering.

a. Tetradecimal
c. Radix
b. Factoradic
d. Hexadecimal

Chapter 2. Equations and Inequalities

13. In mathematics, a _____ is a polynomial equation of the second degree. The general form is

$$ax^2 + bx + c = 0,$$

where a ≠ 0.

The letters a, b, and c are called coefficients: the quadratic coefficient a is the coefficient of x^2, the linear coefficient b is the coefficient of x, and c is the constant coefficient, also called the free term or constant term.

 a. Linear equation
 b. Difference of two squares
 c. Quartic equation
 d. Quadratic equation

14. _____ is an algebraic technique used to solve quadratic equations, in analytic geometry for determining the shapes of graphs, and in calculus for computing integrals. The essential objective is to reduce a quadratic polynomial in a variable in an equation or expression to a squared polynomial of linear order. This can reduce an equation or integral to one that is more easily solved or evaluated.

 a. Relation algebra
 b. Monomial basis
 c. Permanent of a matrix
 d. Completing the square

15. In mathematics, a _____ is a statement that can be proved on the basis of explicitly stated or previously agreed assumptions.

 a. Logical value
 b. Disjunction introduction
 c. Boolean function
 d. Theorem

16. A quadratic equation with real solutions, called roots, which may be real or complex, is given by the _____: $x = \frac{-b \pm \sqrt{b^2 - 4ac}}{2a}$.

 a. Quotient
 b. Parametric continuity
 c. Differential Algebra
 d. Quadratic formula

17. In algebra, the _____ of a polynomial with real or complex coefficients is a certain expression in the coefficients of the polynomial which is equal to zero if and only if the polynomial has a multiple root in the complex numbers. For example, the _____ of the quadratic polynomial

$$ax^2 + bx + c \text{ is } b^2 - 4ac.$$

The _____ of the cubic polynomial

$$ax^3 + bx^2 + cx + d \text{ is } b^2c^2 - 4ac^3 - 4b^3d - 27a^2d^2 + 18abcd.$$

 a. Discriminant
 b. Boubaker polynomial
 c. Jacobian conjecture
 d. Square-free polynomial

18. In mathematics, the _____s are an extension of the real numbers obtained by adjoining an imaginary unit, denoted i, which satisfies:

Chapter 2. Equations and Inequalities

$i^2 = -1.$

Every _____ can be written in the form a + bi, where a and b are real numbers called the real part and the imaginary part of the _____, respectively.

_____s are a field, and thus have addition, subtraction, multiplication, and division operations. These operations extend the corresponding operations on real numbers, although with a number of additional elegant and useful properties, e.g., negative real numbers can be obtained by squaring _____s.

a. 1-center problem
b. Real part
c. 120-cell
d. Complex number

19. In mathematics, an _____ is a complex number whose squared value is a real number less than or equal to zero. The imaginary unit, denoted by i or j, is an example of an _____. If y is a real number, then i·y is an _____, because:

$(i \cdot y)^2 = i^2 \cdot y^2 = -y^2 \leq 0.$

They were defined in 1572 by Rafael Bombelli.

a. A posteriori
b. A Mathematical Theory of Communication
c. A chemical equation
d. Imaginary number

20. In mathematics, the _____ of a complex number z, is the second element of the ordered pair of real numbers representing z,. It is denoted by Im or $\Im\{z\}$, where $\Im$ is a capital I in the Fraktur typeface. The complex function which maps z to the _____ of z is not holomorphic.

a. A posteriori
b. A Mathematical Theory of Communication
c. A chemical equation
d. Imaginary part

21. In mathematics, the _____ of a real number is its numerical value without regard to its sign. So, for example, 3 is the _____ of both 3 and −3.

The _____ of a number a is denoted by $|a|$.

Generalizations of the _____ for real numbers occur in a wide variety of mathematical settings.

a. A chemical equation
b. Area hyperbolic functions
c. A Mathematical Theory of Communication
d. Absolute value

22. In mathematics, an arithmetic progression or _____ is a sequence of numbers such that the difference of any two successive members of the sequence is a constant. For instance, the sequence 3, 5, 7, 9, 11, 13... is an arithmetic progression with common difference 2.

Chapter 2. Equations and Inequalities

a. Arithmetic sequence
b. Alternating series test
c. Edgeworth series
d. Eisenstein series

23. _____ is the mathematical operation of scaling one number by another. It is one of the four basic operations in elementary arithmetic.

_____ is defined for whole numbers in terms of repeated addition; for example, 4 multiplied by 3 can be calculated by adding 3 copies of 4 together:

$$4 + 4 + 4 = 12.$$

_____ of rational numbers and real numbers is defined by systematic generalization of this basic idea.

a. Highest common factor
b. The number 0 is even.
c. Least common multiple
d. Multiplication

24. In mathematics, a _____ is a set of numbers,, together with one or more operations, such as addition or multiplication.

Examples of _____s include: natural numbers, integers, rational numbers, algebraic numbers, real numbers, complex numbers, p-adic numbers, surreal numbers, and hyperreal numbers.

a. Tally marks
b. Number line
c. Slope
d. Number system

25. In mathematics, the _____ of a complex number z, is the first element of the ordered pair of real numbers representing z. It is denoted by Re{z} or $\mathfrak{R}${z}, where $\mathfrak{R}$ is a capital R in the Fraktur typeface. The complex function which maps z to the _____ of z is not holomorphic.

a. 1-center problem
b. 120-cell
c. Complex number
d. Real part

26. In mathematics, the _____s may be described informally in several different ways. The _____s include both rational numbers, such as 42 and −23/129, and irrational numbers, such as pi and the square root of two; or, a _____ can be given by an infinite decimal representation, such as 2.4871773339...., where the digits continue in some way; or, the _____s may be thought of as points on an infinitely long number line.

These descriptions of the _____s, while intuitively accessible, are not sufficiently rigorous for the purposes of pure mathematics.

a. Tally marks
b. Pre-algebra
c. Minkowski distance
d. Real number

Chapter 2. Equations and Inequalities

27. In algebra, a _____ of an element in a quadratic extension field of a field K is its image under the unique non-identity automorphism of the extended field that fixes K. If the extension is generated by a square root of an element r of K, then the _____ of $a + b\sqrt{r}$ is $a - b\sqrt{r}$ for $a, b \in K$, and in particular in the case of the field C of complex numbers as an extension of the field R of real numbers, the complex _____ of a + bi is a − bi.

Forming the sum or product of any element of the extension field with its _____ always gives an element of K.

   a. Real structure
   b. Conjugate
   c. Relation algebra
   d. Trinomial

28. In mathematics, the _____ of a number n is the number that, when added to n, yields zero. The _____ of n is denoted −n. For example, 7 is −7, because 7 + (−7) = 0, and the _____ of −0.3 is 0.3, because −0.3 + 0.3 = 0.
   a. Additive inverse
   b. Algebraic structure
   c. Associativity
   d. Arity

29. In mathematics, a _____ for a number x, denoted by $\frac{1}{x}$ or x^{-1}, is a number which when multiplied by x yields the multiplicative identity, 1. The _____ of x is also called the reciprocal of x. The _____ of a fraction p/q is q/p.
   a. Multiplicative inverse
   b. Hyperbolic function
   c. Double exponential
   d. Golden function

30. In mathematics, a _____ is the end result of a division problem. It can also be expressed as the number of times the divisor divides into the dividend.
   a. Notation
   b. Limiting
   c. Marginal cost
   d. Quotient

31. In mathematics, a _____ of a number x is a number r such that $r^2 = x$, or, in other words, a number r whose square is x. Every non-negative real number x has a unique non-negative _____, called the principal _____, which is denoted with a radical symbol as $\sqrt{x}$, or, using exponent notation, as $x^{1/2}$. For example, the principal _____ of 9 is 3, denoted $\sqrt{9} = 3$, because $3^2 = 3 \times 3 = 9$.
   a. Multiplicative inverse
   b. Double exponential
   c. Hyperbolic functions
   d. Square root

32. A _____ of a number is a number a such that $a^3 = x$.
   a. Golden function
   b. Hyperbolic functions
   c. Square root
   d. Cube root

33. In mathematics, the nth _____ are all the complex numbers which yield 1 when raised to a given power n. It can be shown that they are located on the unit circle of the complex plane and that in that plane they form the vertices of an n-sided regular polygon with one vertex on 1.
   a. Square root of 2
   b. Roots of unity
   c. 120-cell
   d. 1-center problem

34. Exponentiation is a mathematical operation, written a^n, involving two numbers, the base a and the _____ n. When n is a positive integer, exponentiation corresponds to repeated multiplication:

$$a^n = \underbrace{a \times \cdots \times a}_{n},$$

just as multiplication by a positive integer corresponds to repeated addition:

$$a \times n = \underbrace{a + \cdots + a}_{n}.$$

The _____ is usually shown as a superscript to the right of the base. The exponentiation a^n can be read as: a raised to the n-th power, a raised to the power [of] n or possibly a raised to the _____ [of] n, or more briefly: a to the n-th power or a to the power [of] n, or even more briefly: a to the n.

a. Exponent
b. Exponential sum
c. Exponentiating by squaring
d. Exponential tree

35. In mathematics, an algebraic group G contains a unique maximal normal solvable subgroup; and this subgroup is closed. Its identity component is called the _____ of G.
   a. Block size
   b. Composite
   c. Radical
   d. Barycentric coordinates

36. In mathematics, the _____ or Pythagoras' theorem is a relation in Euclidean geometry among the three sides of a right triangle. The theorem is named after the Greek mathematician Pythagoras, who by tradition is credited with its discovery and proof, although it is often argued that knowledge of the theory predates him.. The theorem is as follows:

In any right triangle, the area of the square whose side is the hypotenuse is equal to the sum of the areas of the squares whose sides are the two legs.

   a. 120-cell
   b. 1-center problem
   c. 2-3 heap
   d. Pythagorean theorem

37. In mathematics, an _____ is a statement about the relative size or order of two objects, or about whether they are the same or not

- The notation a < b means that a is less than b.
- The notation a > b means that a is greater than b.
- The notation a ≠ b means that a is not equal to b, but does not say that one is bigger than the other or even that they can be compared in size.

In all these cases, a is not equal to b, hence, '_____'.

These relations are known as strict _____

- The notation a ≤ b means that a is less than or equal to b;
- The notation a ≥ b means that a is greater than or equal to b;

An additional use of the notation is to show that one quantity is much greater than another, normally by several orders of magnitude.

- The notation a << b means that a is much less than b.
- The notation a >> b means that a is much greater than b.

If the sense of the _____ is the same for all values of the variables for which its members are defined, then the _____ is called an 'absolute' or 'unconditional' _____. If the sense of an _____ holds only for certain values of the variables involved, but is reversed or destroyed for other values of the variables, it is called a conditional _____.

An _____ may appear unsolvable because it only states whether a number is larger or smaller than another number; but it is possible to apply the same operations for equalities to inequalities. For example, to find x for the _____ 10x > 23 one would divide 23 by 10.

a. A Mathematical Theory of Communication
b. A chemical equation
c. A posteriori
d. Inequality

38. _____ is the state of being greater than any finite number, however large.
    a. Interval notation
    b. A Mathematical Theory of Communication
    c. Implicit differentiation
    d. Infinity

39. In mathematics, a _____ is a set of real numbers with the property that any number that lies between two numbers in the set is also included in the set. For example, the set of all numbers x satisfying $0 \leq x \leq 1$ is an _____ which contains 0 and 1, as well as all numbers between them. Other examples of _____s are the set of all real numbers $\mathbb{R}$, the set of all positive real numbers, and the empty set.
    a. Ideal
    b. Annihilator
    c. Interval
    d. Order

40. _____ is the magnitude of change in the oscillating variable, with each oscillation, within an oscillating system. For instance, sound waves are oscillations in atmospheric pressure and their _____s are proportional to the change in pressure during one oscillation. If the variable undergoes regular oscillations, and a graph of the system is drawn with the oscillating variable as the vertical axis and time as the horizontal axis, the _____ is visually represented by the vertical distance between the extrema of the curve.
    a. Angular velocity
    b. Angular frequency
    c. Areal velocity
    d. Amplitude

Chapter 2. Equations and Inequalities

41. In mathematics, the concept of a _____ tries to capture the intuitive idea of a geometrical one-dimensional and continuous object. A simple example is the circle. In everyday use of the term '_____', a straight line is not curved, but in mathematical parlance _____s include straight lines and line segments.
   a. Kappa curve
   b. Negative pedal curve
   c. Curve
   d. Quadrifolium

42. In mathematics, the _____ of two sets A and B is the set that contains all elements of A that also belong to B, but no other elements.

For explanation of the symbols used in this article, refer to the table of mathematical symbols.

The _____ of A and B

The _____ of A and B is written 'A ∩ B'. Formally:

   x is an element of A ∩ B if and only if
   - x is an element of A and
   - x is an element of B.
   For example:
   - The _____ of the sets {1, 2, 3} and {2, 3, 4} is {2, 3}.
   - The number 9 is not in the _____ of the set of prime numbers {2, 3, 5, 7, 11, …} and the set of odd numbers {1, 3, 5, 7, 9, 11, …}.

If the _____ of two sets A and B is empty, that is they have no elements in common, then they are said to be disjoint, denoted: A ∩ B = Ø. For example the sets {1, 2} and {3, 4} are disjoint, written {1, 2} ∩ {3, 4} = Ø.

   a. Erlang
   b. Advice
   c. Intersection
   d. Order

43. In set theory, the term _____ refers to a set operation used in the convergence of set elements to form a resultant set containing the elements of both sets. As a simple example, a _____ of two disjoint sets, which do not have elements in common results in a set containing all elements from both sets. A Venn diagram representing the _____ of sets A and B.
   a. Introduction
   b. UES
   c. Event
   d. Union

44. A _____ is a 2D geometric symbolic representation of information according to some visualization technique. Sometimes, the technique uses a 3D visualization which is then projected onto the 2D surface. The word graph is sometimes used as a synonym for _____.
   a. 1-center problem
   b. 120-cell
   c. 2-3 heap
   d. Diagram

Chapter 3. Functions and Graphs

1. The x-axis is the horizontal axis of a two-dimensional plot in the _____, that is typically pointed to the right. Also known as a right-handed coordinate system.
    a. 1-center problem
    b. 120-cell
    c. 2-3 heap
    d. Cartesian coordinate system

2. In mathematics and in the sciences, a _____ (plural: _____e, formulæ or _____s) is a concise way of expressing information symbolically (as in a mathematical or chemical _____), or a general relationship between quantities. One of many famous _____e is Albert Einstein's $E = mc^2$ (see special relativity

In mathematics, a _____ is a key to solve an equation with variables. For example, the problem of determining the volume of a sphere is one that requires a significant amount of integral calculus to solve.

    a. 1-center problem
    b. 2-3 heap
    c. 120-cell
    d. Formula

3. In quantum field theory and statistical mechanics in the thermodynamic limit, a system with a global symmetry can have more than one phase. For parameters where the symmetry is spontaneously broken, the system is said to be _____. When the global symmetry is unbroken the system is disordered.
    a. Ordered
    b. Isoenthalpic-isobaric ensemble
    c. Ursell function
    d. Einstein relation

4. In mathematics, an _____ is a collection of objects having two coordinates (or entries or projections), such that one can always uniquely determine the object, which is the first coordinate (or first entry or left projection) of the pair as well as the second coordinate (or second entry or right projection.) If the first coordinate is a and the second is b, the usual notation for an _____ is (a, b.) The pair is 'ordered' in that (a, b) differs from (b, a) unless a = b.
    a. A Mathematical Theory of Communication
    b. A chemical equation
    c. A posteriori
    d. Ordered pair

5. In mathematics, the _____ of a Euclidean space is a special point, usually denoted by the letter O, used as a fixed point of reference for the geometry of the surrounding space. In a Cartesian coordinate system, the _____ is the point where the axes of the system intersect. In Euclidean geometry, the _____ may be chosen freely as any convenient point of reference.
    a. Autonomous system
    b. OMAC
    c. Interval
    d. Origin

6. A _____ consists of one quarter of the coordinate plane.
    a. 120-cell
    b. 2-3 heap
    c. Quadrant
    d. 1-center problem

7. In mathematics and computer science, _____ (also base-16, hexa or base, of 16. It uses sixteen distinct symbols, most often the symbols 0-9 to represent values zero to nine, and A, B, C, D, E, F (or a through f) to represent values ten to fifteen.

Its primary use is as a human friendly representation of binary coded values, so it is often used in digital electronics and computer engineering.

Chapter 3. Functions and Graphs

a. Hexadecimal
b. Radix
c. Factoradic
d. Tetradecimal

8. In algebra, a _____ of an element in a quadratic extension field of a field K is its image under the unique non-identity automorphism of the extended field that fixes K. If the extension is generated by a square root of an element r of K, then the _____ of $a + b\sqrt{r}$ is $a - b\sqrt{r}$ for $a, b \in K$, and in particular in the case of the field C of complex numbers as an extension of the field R of real numbers, the complex _____ of a + bi is a − bi.

Forming the sum or product of any element of the extension field with its _____ always gives an element of K.

a. Relation algebra
b. Conjugate
c. Trinomial
d. Real structure

9. In mathematics, a _____ is, informally, an infinitely vast and infinitely thin sheet. _____s may be thought of as objects in some higher dimensional space, or they may be considered without any outside space, as in the setting of Euclidean geometry

a. Blocking
b. Bandwidth
c. Group
d. Plane

10. The _____ is the horizontal axis of a two- dimensional plot in the Cartesian coordinate system, that is typically pointed to the right. Also known as a right-handed coordinate system.

a. 1-center problem
b. X-axis
c. 2-3 heap
d. 120-cell

11. The _____ is one of the coordinates of a point in a two or three-dimensional cartesian coordinate system, equal to the distance of a point from the y-axis in a 2D system, or from the plane of y and z axes in a 3D system, measured along a line parallel to the x axis.

a. 1-center problem
b. 2-3 heap
c. 120-cell
d. X-coordinate

12. In reference to a 2D and 3D plane, the _____ is the vertical height of a 2D or 3D object.

a. 1-center problem
b. 120-cell
c. 2-3 heap
d. Y-axis

13. The _____ is the distance between a point and an axis in the Cartesian Coordinate System.

a. 120-cell
b. 2-3 heap
c. 1-center problem
d. Y-coordinate

14. In mathematics, the _____ or Pythagoras' theorem is a relation in Euclidean geometry among the three sides of a right triangle. The theorem is named after the Greek mathematician Pythagoras, who by tradition is credited with its discovery and proof, although it is often argued that knowledge of the theory predates him.. The theorem is as follows:

In any right triangle, the area of the square whose side is the hypotenuse is equal to the sum of the areas of the squares whose sides are the two legs.

a. Pythagorean theorem
b. 1-center problem
c. 2-3 heap
d. 120-cell

15. A _____ is one of the basic shapes of geometry: a polygon with three corners or vertices and three sides or edges which are line segments. A _____ with vertices A, B, and C is denoted ABC.

In Euclidean geometry any three non-collinear points determine a unique _____ and a unique plane.

   a. 1-center problem
   b. Fuhrmann circle
   c. Triangle
   d. Kepler triangle

16. _____ is a quantity expressing the two-dimensional size of a defined part of a surface, typically a region bounded by a closed curve. The term surface _____ refers to the total _____ of the exposed surface of a 3-dimensional solid, such as the sum of the _____s of the exposed sides of a polyhedron. _____ is an important invariant in the differential geometry of surfaces.
   a. A chemical equation
   b. A Mathematical Theory of Communication
   c. A posteriori
   d. Area

17. In mathematics, a _____ is a statement that can be proved on the basis of explicitly stated or previously agreed assumptions.
   a. Boolean function
   b. Theorem
   c. Disjunction introduction
   d. Logical value

18. In mathematics, the _____s are analogs of the ordinary trigonometric functions. The basic _____s are the hyperbolic sine 'sinh', and the hyperbolic cosine 'cosh', from which are derived the hyperbolic tangent 'tanh', etc., in analogy to the derived trigonometric functions. The inverse _____ are the area hyperbolic sine 'arsinh' (also called 'asinh', or sometimes by the misnomer of 'arcsinh') and so on.
   a. Heaviside step function
   b. Square root
   c. Rectangular function
   d. Hyperbolic function

19. A _____ or circle sector, is the portion of a circle enclosed by two radii and an arc, where the smaller area is known as the minor sector and the larger being the major sector. Its area can be calculated as described below.

Let θ be the central angle, in radians, and r the radius.

   a. Circumcircle
   b. Circular segment
   c. Circumscribed circle
   d. Circular sector

20. _____ is the magnitude of change in the oscillating variable, with each oscillation, within an oscillating system. For instance, sound waves are oscillations in atmospheric pressure and their _____s are proportional to the change in pressure during one oscillation. If the variable undergoes regular oscillations, and a graph of the system is drawn with the oscillating variable as the vertical axis and time as the horizontal axis, the _____ is visually represented by the vertical distance between the extrema of the curve.
   a. Angular velocity
   b. Angular frequency
   c. Areal velocity
   d. Amplitude

Chapter 3. Functions and Graphs

21. In mathematics, the _____ is a conic section, the intersection of a right circular conical surface and a plane parallel to a generating straight line of that surface. Given a point and a line that lie in a plane, the locus of points in that plane that are equidistant to them is a _____.

A particular case arises when the plane is tangent to the conical surface of a circle.

   a. Matrix representation of conic sections   b. Dandelin sphere
   c. Directrix   d. Parabola

22. In geometry, a _____ is a special kind of point, usually a corner of a polygon, polyhedron, or higher dimensional polytope. In the geometry of curves a _____ is a point of where the first derivative of curvature is zero. In graph theory, a _____ is the fundamental unit out of which graphs are formed
   a. Crib   b. Duality
   c. Dini   d. Vertex

23. In geometry and trigonometry, an _____ is the figure formed by two rays sharing a common endpoint, called the vertex of the _____. The magnitude of the _____ is the 'amount of rotation' that separates the two rays, and can be measured by considering the length of circular arc swept out when one ray is rotated about the vertex to coincide with the other. Where there is no possibility of confusion, the term '_____' is used interchangeably for both the geometric configuration itself and for its angular magnitude.
   a. A posteriori   b. A chemical equation
   c. A Mathematical Theory of Communication   d. Angle

24. The mathematical concept of a _____ expresses the intuitive idea of deterministic dependence between two quantities, one of which is viewed as primary and the other as secondary. A _____ then is a way to associate a unique output for each input of a specified type, for example, a real number or an element of a given set.
   a. Coherent   b. Going up
   c. Grill   d. Function

25. In vascular plants, the _____ is the organ of a plant body that typically lies below the surface of the soil. This is not always the case, however, since a _____ can also be aerial (that is, growing above the ground) or aerating (that is, growing up above the ground or especially above water.) Furthermore, a stem normally occurring below ground is not exceptional either
   a. 120-cell   b. Root
   c. 2-3 heap   d. 1-center problem

26. A _____ is a mirror based duplicate of a single image. _____

In geometry, the _____ of an object or two-dimensional figure is the virtual image formed by reflection in a plane mirror; it is of the same size as the original object, yet different, unless the object or figure has reflection symmetry.

If a point of an object has coordinates then the image of this point has coordinates - so mirror reflection is a reversal of the coordinate axis perpendicular to the mirror's surface.

Chapter 3. Functions and Graphs

a. Perimeter
c. Shape

b. Golden angle
d. Mirror image

27. An _____ is an artifact, usually two-dimensional (a picture), that has a similar appearance to some subject--usually a physical object or a person.

_____s may be two-dimensional, such as a photograph, screen display, and as well as a three-dimensional, such as a statue. They may be captured by optical devices--such as cameras, mirrors, lenses, telescopes, microscopes, etc.

a. Image
c. A Mathematical Theory of Communication

b. A posteriori
d. A chemical equation

28. _____ generally conveys two primary meanings. The first is an imprecise sense of harmonious or aesthetically-pleasing proportionality and balance; such that it reflects beauty or perfection. The second meaning is a precise and well-defined concept of balance or 'patterned self-similarity' that can be demonstrated or proved according to the rules of a formal system: by geometry, through physics or otherwise.

a. Tessellation
c. Molecular symmetry

b. Symmetry breaking
d. Symmetry

29. A _____ is a simple shape of Euclidean geometry consisting of those points in a plane which are at a constant distance, called the radius, from a fixed point, called the center. A _____ with center A is sometimes denoted by the symbol A.

A chord of a _____ is a line segment whose two endpoints lie on the _____.

a. Malfatti circles
c. Circle

b. Circular segment
d. Circumcircle

30. _____ is an algebraic technique used to solve quadratic equations, in analytic geometry for determining the shapes of graphs, and in calculus for computing integrals. The essential objective is to reduce a quadratic polynomial in a variable in an equation or expression to a squared polynomial of linear order. This can reduce an equation or integral to one that is more easily solved or evaluated.

a. Permanent of a matrix
c. Monomial basis

b. Relation algebra
d. Completing the square

31. In mathematics, a _____ is a circle with a unit radius. Frequently, especially in trigonometry, 'the' _____ is the circle of radius 1 centered at the origin in the Cartesian coordinate system in the Euclidean plane. The _____ is often denoted S^1; the generalization to higher dimensions is the unit sphere.

a. Excircle
c. Inscribed angle theorem

b. Open unit disk
d. Unit circle

32. The term _____ or centre is used in various contexts in abstract algebra to denote the set of all those elements that commute with all other elements. More specifically:

- The _____ of a group G consists of all those elements x in G such that xg = gx for all g in G. This is a normal subgroup of G.
- The _____ of a ring R is the subset of R consisting of all those elements x of R such that xr = rx for all r in R. The _____ is a commutative subring of R, so R is an algebra over its _____.
- The _____ of an algebra A consists of all those elements x of A such that xa = ax for all a in A. See also: central simple algebra.
- The _____ of a Lie algebra L consists of all those elements x in L such that [x,a] = 0 for all a in L. This is an ideal of the Lie algebra L.
- The _____ of a monoidal category C consists of pairs *a natural isomorphism satisfying certain axioms*.

a. Disk
b. Block size
c. Brute Force
d. Center

33. In classical geometry, a _____ of a circle or sphere is any line segment from its center to its boundary. By extension, the _____ of a circle or sphere is the length of any such segment. The _____ is half the diameter. In science and engineering the term _____ of curvature is commonly used as a synonym for _____.

a. Radius
b. Birational geometry
c. Duoprism
d. Non-Euclidean geometry

34. In mathematics, a _____ is a two-dimensional geometric shape that forms half of a circle. Being half of a circle's 360°, the arc of a _____ always measures 180°. A triangle inscribed in a _____ is always a right triangle.

a. Parallel lines
b. Medial triangle
c. Spidron
d. Semicircle

35. _____ is used to describe the steepness, incline, gradient, or grade of a straight line. A higher _____ value indicates a steeper incline. The _____ is defined as the ratio of the 'rise' divided by the 'run' between two points on a line, or in other words, the ratio of the altitude change to the horizontal distance between any two points on the line.

a. Number line
b. Cognitively Guided Instruction
c. Slope
d. Point plotting

36. In mathematics, the _____ of a real number is its numerical value without regard to its sign. So, for example, 3 is the _____ of both 3 and −3.

The _____ of a number a is denoted by $|a|$.

Generalizations of the _____ for real numbers occur in a wide variety of mathematical settings.

a. A chemical equation
b. A Mathematical Theory of Communication
c. Area hyperbolic functions
d. Absolute value

Chapter 3. Functions and Graphs

37. In mathematics, the _____ is an approach to finding a particular solution to certain inhomogeneous ordinary differential equations and recurrence relations. It is closely related to the annihilator method, but instead of using a particular kind of differential operator in order to find the best possible form of the particular solution, a 'guess' is made as to the appropriate form, which is then tested by differentiating the resulting equation. In this sense, the _____ is less formal but more intuitive than the annihilator method.
   a. Differential algebraic equations
   b. Linear differential equation
   c. Phase line
   d. Method of undetermined coefficients

38. The _____ expresses the fact that the difference in the y coordinate between two points on a line that is, y − y1 is proportional to the difference in the x coordinate that is, x − x1. The proportionality constant is m (the slope of the line.
   a. Rubin Causal Model
   b. Square function
   c. Cobb-Douglas
   d. Point-slope form

39. A _____ is an algebraic equation in which each term is either a constant or the product of a constant and a single variable. _____s can have one, two, three or more variables.

   _____s occur with great regularity in applied mathematics.

   a. Quartic equation
   b. Quadratic equation
   c. Difference of two squares
   d. Linear equation

40. _____ is a form where m is the slope of the line and b is the y-intercept, which is the y-coordinate of the point where the line crosses the y axis. This can be seen by letting x = 0, which immediately gives y = b.
   a. Separable extension
   b. Dynamical system
   c. Commutative law
   d. Slope-intercept form

41. A _____ of a curve is the envelope of a family of congruent circles centered on the curve. It generalises the concept of _____ lines.

   It is sometimes called the offset curve but the term 'offset' often refers also to translation.

   a. Cycloid
   b. Bifolium
   c. Cissoid
   d. Parallel

42. The existence and properties of _____ are the basis of Euclid's parallel postulate. _____ are two lines on the same plane that do not intersect even assuming that lines extend to infinity in either direction.
   a. Square wheel
   b. Vertical translation
   c. Spidron
   d. Parallel lines

43. A _____ is an abstract model that uses mathematical language to describe the behavior of a system. Eykhoff defined a _____ as 'a representation of the essential aspects of an existing system which presents knowledge of that system in usable form'.
   a. Total least squares
   b. Rata Die
   c. Mathematical model
   d. Metaheuristic

44. In mathematics, especially in the area of abstract algebra known as ring theory, a _____ is a ring with 0 ≠ 1 such that ab = 0 implies that either a = 0 or b = 0. That is, it is a nontrivial ring without left or right zero divisors. A commutative _____ is called an integral _____.

   a. Simple ring
   b. Modular representation theory
   c. Left primitive ring
   d. Domain

45. In descriptive statistics, the _____ is the length of the smallest interval which contains all the data. It is calculated by subtracting the smallest observations from the greatest and provides an indication of statistical dispersion.

It is measured in the same units as the data.

   a. Bandwidth
   b. Kernel
   c. Class
   d. Range

46. In abstract algebra, a field extension L /K is called _____ if every element of L is _____ over K. Field extensions which are not _____.

For example, the field extension R/Q, that is the field of real numbers as an extension of the field of rational numbers, is transcendental, while the field extensions C/R and Q

   a. Ideal
   b. Identity
   c. Echo
   d. Algebraic

47. In mathematics, _____ and undefined are used to explain whether or not expressions have meaningful, sensible, and unambiguous values. Not all branches of mathematics come to the same conclusion.

The following expressions are undefined in all contexts, but remarks in the analysis section may apply.

   a. Plugging in
   b. LHS
   c. Toy model
   d. Defined

48. A _____ of a number is a number a such that $a^3 = x$.

   a. Hyperbolic functions
   b. Golden function
   c. Square root
   d. Cube root

49. In mathematics, a _____ of a number x is a number r such that $r^2 = x$, or, in other words, a number r whose square is x. Every non-negative real number x has a unique non-negative _____, called the principal _____, which is denoted with a radical symbol as $\sqrt{x}$, or, using exponent notation, as $x^{1/2}$. For example, the principal _____ of 9 is 3, denoted $\sqrt{9}$ = 3, because $3^2 = 3 \times 3 = 9$.

   a. Multiplicative inverse
   b. Double exponential
   c. Hyperbolic functions
   d. Square root

50. In mathematics, a _____ is a function whose values do not vary and thus are constant. For example, if we have the function f→ B is a _____ if f

Chapter 3. Functions and Graphs

a. Constant function
c. Linear operator
b. Squeeze mapping
d. Point reflection

51. In calculus, a function f defined on a subset of the real numbers with real values is called monotonic (also monotonically increasing or non-_____), if for all x and y such that x ≤ y one has f(x) ≤ f(y), so f preserves the order. In layman's terms, the sign of the slope is always positive (the curve tending upwards) or zero (i.e., non-_____, or asymptotic, or depicted as a horizontal, flat line) Likewise, a function is called monotonically _____ (non-increasing) if, whenever x ≤ y, then f(x) ≥ f(y), so it reverses the order.

a. Tensor product of Hilbert spaces
c. Circular convolution
b. Dual pair
d. Decreasing

52. In mathematics, the term _____ has several different important meanings:

- An _____ is an equality that remains true regardless of the values of any variables that appear within it, to distinguish it from an equality which is true under more particular conditions. For this, the 'triple bar' symbol ≡ is sometimes used.
- In algebra, an _____ or _____ element of a set S with a binary operation Â· is an element e that, when combined with any element x of S, produces that same x. That is, eÂ·x = xÂ·e = x for all x in S.
    - The _____ function from a set S to itself, often denoted id or id$_S$, s the function such that i = x for all x in S. This function serves as the _____ element in the set of all functions from S to itself with respect to function composition.
    - In linear algebra, the _____ matrix of size n is the n-by-n square matrix with ones on the main diagonal and zeros elsewhere. This matrix serves as the _____ with respect to matrix multiplication.

A common example of the first meaning is the trigonometric _____

$$\sin^2 \theta + \cos^2 \theta = 1$$

which is true for all real values of θ, as opposed to

$$\cos \theta = 1,$$

which is true only for some values of θ, not all. For example, the latter equation is true when $\theta = 0$, false when $\theta = 2$

The concepts of 'additive _____' and 'multiplicative _____' are central to the Peano axioms. The number 0 is the 'additive _____' for integers, real numbers, and complex numbers. For the real numbers, for all $a \in \mathbb{R}$,

$$0 + a = a,$$

$$a + 0 = a, \text{ and}$$

$$0 + 0 = 0.$$

Similarly, The number 1 is the 'multiplicative _____' for integers, real numbers, and complex numbers.

   a. Identity
   c. Action
   b. ARIA
   d. Intersection

53. An _____ is a function that does not have any effect: it always returns the same value that was used as its argument.
   a. Inverse function
   c. Algebra
   b. Angle bisector
   d. Identity function

54. In mathematics, a _____ is the end result of a division problem. It can also be expressed as the number of times the divisor divides into the dividend.
   a. Notation
   c. Marginal cost
   b. Limiting
   d. Quotient

55. _____ and independent variables refer to values that change in relationship to each other. The _____ are those that are observed to change in response to the independent variables. The independent variables are those that are deliberately manipulated to invoke a change in the _____.
   a. Yates analysis
   c. Round robin test
   b. Steiner system
   d. Dependent variables

56. Dependent variables and _____ refer to values that change in relationship to each other. The dependent variables are those that are observed to change in response to the _____. The _____ are those that are deliberately manipulated to invoke a change in the dependent variables.
   a. One-factor-at-a-time method
   c. Experimental design diagram
   b. Independent variables
   d. Operational confound

57. In mathematics, even functions and _____s are functions which satisfy particular symmetry relations, with respect to taking additive inverses. They are important in many areas of mathematical analysis, especially the theory of power series and Fourier series. They are named for the parity of the powers of the power functions which satisfy each condition: the function f(x) = x^n is an even function if n is an even integer, and it is an _____ if n is an odd integer.
   a. A chemical equation
   c. A posteriori
   b. A Mathematical Theory of Communication
   d. Odd function

58. _____ is the interpreting of the meaning of a text and the subsequent production of an equivalent text, likewise called a '_____,' that communicates the same message in another language. The text to be translated is called the 'source text,' and the language that it is to be translated into is called the 'target language'; the final product is sometimes called the 'target text.'

_____ must take into account constraints that include context, the rules of grammar of the two languages, their writing conventions, and their idioms. A common misconception is that there exists a simple word-for-word correspondence between any two languages, and that _____ is a straightforward mechanical process; such a word-for-word _____, however, cannot take into account context, grammar, conventions, and idioms.

a. 1-center problem
b. 2-3 heap
c. 120-cell
d. Translation

59. In functional analysis, the _____ of a linear operator T on a Hilbert space to a subspace K is the operator

$$P_K T|_K$$

where P_K is the orthogonal projection onto K. This is a natural way to obtain an operator on K from an operator on the whole Hilbert space. If K is an invariant subspace for T, then the _____ of T to K is the restricted operator K→K sending k to Tk.

a. Dini
b. Figure-eight knot
c. Center
d. Compression

60. In mathematics, a _____ is a function whose definition is dependent on the value of the independent variable. Mathematically, a real-valued function f of a real variable x is a relationship whose definition is given differently on disjoint subsets of its domain

The word piecewise is also used to describe any property of a _____ that holds for each piece but may not hold for the whole domain of the function.

a. Glide reflection
b. Surjective
c. High-dimensional model representation
d. Piecewise-defined function

61. The _____ are the set of numbers consisting of the natural numbers including 0 and their negatives. They are numbers that can be written without a fractional or decimal component, and fall within the set {... −2, −1, 0, 1, 2, ...}.
a. Integers
b. A chemical equation
c. A Mathematical Theory of Communication
d. A posteriori

62. In algebra, a _____ is a function depending on n that associates a scalar, de, to every n×n square matrix A. The fundamental geometric meaning of a _____ is as the scale factor for measure when A is regarded as a linear transformation. _____s are important both in calculus, where they enter the substitution rule for several variables, and in multilinear algebra.

a. Pfaffian
c. Functional determinant
b. 1-center problem
d. Determinant

63. A _____, in mathematics, is a polynomial function of the form $f(x) = ax^2 + bx + c$, where $a \neq 0$. The graph of a _____ is a parabola whose major axis is parallel to the y-axis.

The expression ax² + bx + c in the definition of a _____ is a polynomial of degree 2 or a 2nd degree polynomial, because the highest exponent of x is 2.

a. Multivariate division algorithm
c. Laguerre polynomials
b. Discriminant
d. Quadratic function

64. In mathematics, an arithmetic progression or _____ is a sequence of numbers such that the difference of any two successive members of the sequence is a constant. For instance, the sequence 3, 5, 7, 9, 11, 13... is an arithmetic progression with common difference 2.

a. Alternating series test
c. Arithmetic sequence
b. Eisenstein series
d. Edgeworth series

65. In mathematics, the _____s are an extension of the real numbers obtained by adjoining an imaginary unit, denoted i, which satisfies:

$$i^2 = -1.$$

Every _____ can be written in the form a + bi, where a and b are real numbers called the real part and the imaginary part of the _____, respectively.

_____s are a field, and thus have addition, subtraction, multiplication, and division operations. These operations extend the corresponding operations on real numbers, although with a number of additional elegant and useful properties, e.g., negative real numbers can be obtained by squaring _____s.

a. 1-center problem
c. Real part
b. Complex number
d. 120-cell

66. In mathematics, an _____ is informally a function which satisfies a polynomial equation whose coefficients are themselves polynomials. For example, an _____ in one variable x is a solution y for an equation

$$a_n(x)y^n + a_{n-1}(x)y^{n-1} + \cdots + a_0(x) = 0$$

where the coefficients a_i

a. Algebraic function
c. Algebraic solution
b. Algebraic signal processing
d. Alternatization

67. A _____ number is a positive integer which has a positive divisor other than one or itself. By definition, every integer greater than one is either a prime number or a _____ number. zero and one are considered to be neither prime nor _____. For example, the integer 14 is a _____ number because it can be factored as 2 × 7.

 a. Discontinuity
 b. Key server
 c. Basis
 d. Composite

68. In mathematics, a _____ is an expression constructed from variables and constants, using the operations of addition, subtraction, multiplication, and constant non-negative whole number exponents. For example, $x^2 - 4x + 7$ is a _____, but $x^2 - 4/x + 7x^{3/2}$ is not, because its second term involves division by the variable x and also because its third term contains an exponent that is not a whole number.

_____s are one of the most important concepts in algebra and throughout mathematics and science.

 a. Semifield
 b. Coimage
 c. Group extension
 d. Polynomial

69. A _____ is a function that does not satisfy a polynomial equation whose coefficients are themselves polynomials, in contrast to an algebraic function, which does satisfy such an equation. In other words a _____ is a function which 'transcends' algebra in the sense that it cannot be expressed in terms of a finite sequence of the algebraic operations of addition, multiplication, and root extraction.

Examples of _____s include the exponential function, the logarithm, and the trigonometric functions.

 a. 120-cell
 b. 1-center problem
 c. 2-3 heap
 d. Transcendental function

Chapter 4. Polynomial and Rational Functions

1. In probability theory, a probability distribution is called _____ if its cumulative distribution function is _____. That is equivalent to saying that for random variables X with the distribution in question, Pr[X = a] = 0 for all real numbers a. If the distribution of X is _____ then X is called a _____ random variable.
   - a. Continuous phase modulation
   - b. Conull set
   - c. Concatenated codes
   - d. Continuous

2. In mathematics, a _____ is a function for which, intuitively, small changes in the input result in small changes in the output. Otherwise, a function is said to be discontinuous. A _____ with a continuous inverse function is called bicontinuous.
   - a. Continuous function
   - b. Beth numbers
   - c. Charles's Law
   - d. Contraction mapping

3. The mathematical concept of a _____ expresses the intuitive idea of deterministic dependence between two quantities, one of which is viewed as primary and the other as secondary. A _____ then is a way to associate a unique output for each input of a specified type, for example, a real number or an element of a given set.
   - a. Going up
   - b. Grill
   - c. Coherent
   - d. Function

4. In mathematics, a _____ is an expression constructed from variables and constants, using the operations of addition, subtraction, multiplication, and constant non-negative whole number exponents. For example, $x^2 - 4x + 7$ is a _____, but $x^2 - 4/x + 7x^{3/2}$ is not, because its second term involves division by the variable x and also because its third term contains an exponent that is not a whole number.

   _____s are one of the most important concepts in algebra and throughout mathematics and science.

   - a. Semifield
   - b. Group extension
   - c. Coimage
   - d. Polynomial

5. In mathematics, the _____ of a real number is its numerical value without regard to its sign. So, for example, 3 is the _____ of both 3 and −3.

   The _____ of a number a is denoted by $|a|$.

   Generalizations of the _____ for real numbers occur in a wide variety of mathematical settings.

   - a. A Mathematical Theory of Communication
   - b. Area hyperbolic functions
   - c. A chemical equation
   - d. Absolute value

Chapter 4. Polynomial and Rational Functions

6. In mathematical analysis, the _____ states that for each value between the least upper bound and greatest lower bound of the image of a continuous function there is a corresponding value in its domain mapping to the original. _____

- Version I. The _____ states the following: If the function y = f∈ [a, b] such that f

- Version II. Suppose that I is an interval [a, b] in the real numbers R and that f : I → R is a continuous function. Then the image set f

    f⊇ [f or f(I) ⊇ [f(b), f(a)].

It is frequently stated in the following equivalent form: Suppose that f : [a, b] → R is continuous and that u is a real number satisfying f(a) < u < f(b) or f(a) > u > f(b.) Then for some c ∈ [a, b], f(c) = u.

This captures an intuitive property of continuous functions: given f continuous on [1, 2], if f(1) = 3 and f(2) = 5 then f must take the value 4 somewhere between 1 and 2.

- a. Uniformly continuous
- b. A Mathematical Theory of Communication
- c. Intermediate value theorem
- d. Equicontinuous

7. _____ is the magnitude of change in the oscillating variable, with each oscillation, within an oscillating system. For instance, sound waves are oscillations in atmospheric pressure and their _____ s are proportional to the change in pressure during one oscillation. If the variable undergoes regular oscillations, and a graph of the system is drawn with the oscillating variable as the vertical axis and time as the horizontal axis, the _____ is visually represented by the vertical distance between the extrema of the curve.
- a. Areal velocity
- b. Angular velocity
- c. Amplitude
- d. Angular frequency

8. In mathematics, a _____ is a statement that can be proved on the basis of explicitly stated or previously agreed assumptions.
- a. Boolean function
- b. Logical value
- c. Disjunction introduction
- d. Theorem

9. In mathematics, a _____ is the end result of a division problem. It can also be expressed as the number of times the divisor divides into the dividend.
- a. Limiting
- b. Marginal cost
- c. Quotient
- d. Notation

10. In mathematics, computing, linguistics and related subjects, an _____ is a sequence of finite instructions, often used for calculation and data processing. It is formally a type of effective method in which a list of well-defined instructions for completing a task will, when given an initial state, proceed through a well-defined series of successive states, eventually terminating in an end-state. The transition from one state to the next is not necessarily deterministic; some _____ s, known as probabilistic _____ s, incorporate randomness.
- a. Algorithm
- b. Out-of-core
- c. Approximate counting algorithm
- d. In-place algorithm

11. In linear algebra a matrix is in _____ if

   - All nonzero rows are above any rows of all zeroes, and
   - The leading coefficient of a row is always strictly to the right of the leading coefficient of the row above it.

This is the definition used in this article, but some texts add a third condition:

   - The leading coefficient of each nonzero row is one.

A matrix is in reduced _____ if it satisfies the above three conditions, and if, in addition

   - Every leading coefficient is the only nonzero entry in its column.

The first non-zero entry in each row is called a pivot.

This matrix is in reduced _____:

$$\begin{bmatrix} 0 & 1 & 4 & 0 & 0 \\ 0 & 0 & 0 & 1 & 0 \\ 0 & 0 & 0 & 0 & 1 \\ 0 & 0 & 0 & 0 & 0 \end{bmatrix}.$$

The following matrix is also in _____, but not in reduced row form:

$$\begin{bmatrix} 1 & 1 & 1 & 1 \\ 0 & 9 & 0 & 2 \\ 0 & 0 & 0 & 3 \end{bmatrix}.$$

However, this matrix is not in _____, as the leading coefficient of row 3 is not strictly to the right of the leading coefficient of row 2.

$$\begin{bmatrix} 1 & 2 & 3 & 4 \\ 0 & 3 & 7 & 2 \\ 0 & 2 & 0 & 0 \end{bmatrix}$$

Every non-zero matrix can be reduced to an infinite number of echelon forms via elementary matrix transformations.

Chapter 4. Polynomial and Rational Functions

a. Gaussian elimination
b. Portable, Extensible Toolkit for Scientific Computation
c. Row echelon form
d. Reduced row echelon form

12. In mathematics, a _____ is a rectangular table of elements, which may be numbers or, more generally, any abstract quantities that can be added and multiplied. Matrices are used to describe linear equations, keep track of the coefficients of linear transformations and to record data that depend on multiple parameters. Matrices are described by the field of _____ theory.
 a. Double counting
 b. Compression
 c. Matrix
 d. Coherent

13. In mathematical analysis, a metric space M is said to be _____ (or Cauchy) if every Cauchy sequence of points in M has a limit that is also in M or alternatively if every Cauchy sequence in M converges in M.

Intuitively, a space is _____ if there are no 'points missing' from it (inside or at the boundary.) For instance, the set of rational numbers is not _____, because $\sqrt{2}$ is 'missing' from it, even though one can construct a Cauchy sequence of rational numbers that converges to it.

 a. 1-center problem
 b. 2-3 heap
 c. 120-cell
 d. Complete

14. In mathematics, the _____ states that every non-constant single-variable polynomial with complex coefficients has at least one complex root. Equivalently, the field of complex numbers is algebraically closed.

Sometimes, this theorem is stated as: every non-zero single-variable polynomial, with complex coefficients, has exactly as many complex roots as its degree, if each root is counted up to its multiplicity.

 a. Closure with a twist
 b. Near-semiring
 c. Fundamental theorem of algebra
 d. Distributive

15. The word _____ has many distinct meanings in different fields of knowledge, depending on their methodologies and the context of discussion. Broadly speaking we can say that a _____ is some kind of belief or claim that (supposedly) explains, asserts, or consolidates some class of claims. Additionally, in contrast with a theorem the statement of the _____ is generally accepted only in some tentative fashion as opposed to regarding it as having been conclusively established.
 a. Defined
 b. Transport of structure
 c. Per mil
 d. Theory

16. In mathematics, the _____ comprises a major part of traditional algebra. Topics include polynomials, algebraic equations, separation of roots including Sturm's theorem, approximation of roots, and the application of matrices and determinants to the solving of equations.

From the point of view of abstract algebra, the material is divided between symmetric function theory, field theory, Galois theory, and computational considerations including numerical analysis.

a. Theory of equations
b. Relation algebra
c. Laws of Form
d. Digital root

17. In mathematics, a _____ is a number that can be expressed as an integral of an algebraic function over an algebraic domain. Kontsevich and Zagier define a _____ as a complex number whose real and imaginary parts are values of absolutely convergent integrals of rational functions with rational coefficients, over domains in given by polynomial inequalities with rational coefficients.
    a. Boussinesq approximation
    b. Disk
    c. Closeness
    d. Period

18. In vascular plants, the _____ is the organ of a plant body that typically lies below the surface of the soil. This is not always the case, however, since a _____ can also be aerial (that is, growing above the ground) or aerating (that is, growing up above the ground or especially above water.) Furthermore, a stem normally occurring below ground is not exceptional either
    a. 2-3 heap
    b. 120-cell
    c. 1-center problem
    d. Root

19. In mathematics, the _____ of a polynomial is the term of degree 0. For example, in the polynomial

    $X^3 + 2X + 3$

over the variable X, the _____ is 3. Here, the _____ is given by a numeral, but it may also be specified by a letter that is a parameter rather than a variable, as in the polynomial

    $ax^2 + bx + c,$

in the variable x, where a, b, and c are parameters so that c is the _____.

    a. Jacobian conjecture
    b. Constant term
    c. Sheffer sequence
    d. Stability radius

20. In mathematics, especially in order theory, an upper bound of a subset S of some partially ordered set is an element of P which is greater than or equal to every element of S. The term _____ is defined dually as an element of P which is lesser than or equal to every element of S. A set with an upper bound is said to be bounded from above by that bound, a set with a _____ is said to be bounded from below by that bound.
    a. Lower bound
    b. Cofinality
    c. Partially ordered set
    d. Monomial order

21. In mathematics, especially in order theory, an _____ of a subset S of some partially ordered set is an element of P which is greater than or equal to every element of S. The term lower bound is defined dually as an element of P which is lesser than or equal to every element of S. A set with an _____ is said to be bounded from above by that bound, a set with a lower bound is said to be bounded from below by that bound.
    a. Infinite descending chain
    b. Order isomorphism
    c. Order-embedding
    d. Upper bound

Chapter 4. Polynomial and Rational Functions

22. In algebra, a _____ of an element in a quadratic extension field of a field K is its image under the unique non-identity automorphism of the extended field that fixes K. If the extension is generated by a square root of an element r of K, then the _____ of $a + b\sqrt{r}$ is $a - b\sqrt{r}$ for $a, b \in K$, and in particular in the case of the field C of complex numbers as an extension of the field R of real numbers, the complex _____ of a + bi is a − bi.

Forming the sum or product of any element of the extension field with its _____ always gives an element of K.

a. Real structure
b. Conjugate
c. Trinomial
d. Relation algebra

23. In mathematics, a _____ is any function which can be written as the ratio of two polynomial functions. _____ of degree 2 :

$$y = \frac{x^2 - 3x - 2}{x^2 - 4}$$

In the case of one variable, x, a _____ is a function of the form

$$f(x) = \frac{P(x)}{Q(x)}$$

where P and Q are polynomial function in x and Q is not the zero polynomial. The domain of f is the set of all points x for which the denominator Q

a. 1-center problem
b. Legendre rational functions
c. 120-cell
d. Rational function

24. In mathematics, especially in the area of abstract algebra known as ring theory, a _____ is a ring with 0 ≠ 1 such that ab = 0 implies that either a = 0 or b = 0. That is, it is a nontrivial ring without left or right zero divisors. A commutative _____ is called an integral _____.

a. Left primitive ring
b. Modular representation theory
c. Domain
d. Simple ring

25. In abstract algebra, a field extension L /K is called _____ if every element of L is _____ over K. Field extensions which are not _____.

For example, the field extension R/Q, that is the field of real numbers as an extension of the field of rational numbers, is transcendental, while the field extensions C/R and Q

a. Identity
b. Algebraic
c. Ideal
d. Echo

26. An _____ of a real-valued function y = f(x) is a curve which describes the behavior of f as either x or y tends to infinity.

In other words, as one moves along the graph of f(x) in some direction, the distance between it and the _____ eventually becomes smaller than any distance that one may specify.

If a curve A has the curve B as an _____, one says that A is asymptotic to B. Similarly B is asymptotic to A, so A and B are called asymptotic.

a. Isoperimetric dimension
c. Improper integral
b. Infinite product
d. Asymptote

27. _____ is the state of being greater than any finite number, however large.
a. Implicit differentiation
c. A Mathematical Theory of Communication
b. Interval notation
d. Infinity

28. Suppose f is a function. Then the line y = a is a _____ for f if

$$\lim_{x \to \infty} f(x) = a \text{ or } \lim_{x \to -\infty} f(x) = a.$$

Intuitively, this means that f(x) can be made as close as desired to a by making x big enough. How big is big enough depends on how close one wishes to make f(x) to a.

a. 1-center problem
c. 2-3 heap
b. Horizontal asymptote
d. 120-cell

29. In mathematics, the multiplicative inverse of a number x, denoted 1/x or x^{-1}, is the number which, when multiplied by x, yields 1. The multiplicative inverse of x is also called the _____ of x.
a. 1-center problem
c. 2-3 heap
b. 120-cell
d. Reciprocal

30. _____ is a special mathematical relationship between two quantities. Two quantities are called proportional if they vary in such a way that one of the quantities is a constant multiple of the other, or equivalently if they have a constant ratio.
a. Compression
c. Discontinuity
b. Depth
d. Proportionality

31. In mathematics, the _____ of a number n is the number that, when added to n, yields zero. The _____ of n is denoted −n. For example, 7 is −7, because 7 + (−7) = 0, and the _____ of −0.3 is 0.3, because −0.3 + 0.3 = 0.
a. Associativity
c. Algebraic structure
b. Arity
d. Additive inverse

32. In mathematics, two quantities are called _____ if they vary in such a way that one of the quantities is a constant multiple of the other, or equivalently if they have a constant ratio.
a. 1-center problem
c. 2-3 heap
b. Proportional
d. 120-cell

Chapter 5. Inverse, Exponential, and Logarithmic Functions

1. The mathematical concept of a _____ expresses the intuitive idea of deterministic dependence between two quantities, one of which is viewed as primary and the other as secondary. A _____ then is a way to associate a unique output for each input of a specified type, for example, a real number or an element of a given set.
   a. Coherent
   b. Grill
   c. Going up
   d. Function

2. In mathematics, the _____ of a number n is the number that, when added to n, yields zero. The _____ of n is denoted −n. For example, 7 is −7, because 7 + (−7) = 0, and the _____ of −0.3 is 0.3, because −0.3 + 0.3 = 0.
   a. Algebraic structure
   b. Associativity
   c. Additive inverse
   d. Arity

3. An _____ is a function which does the reverse of a given function.
   a. Empty function
   b. Inverse function
   c. Empty set
   d. A Mathematical Theory of Communication

4. An injective function is called an injection, and is also said to be a _____ (not to be confused with one-to-one correspondence, i.e. a bijective function.)

   A function f that is not injective is sometimes called many-to-one. (However, this terminology is also sometimes used to mean 'single-valued', i.e. each argument is mapped to at most one value.)

   a. A chemical equation
   b. A Mathematical Theory of Communication
   c. A posteriori
   d. One-to-one function

5. In mathematics, the _____ of a real number is its numerical value without regard to its sign. So, for example, 3 is the _____ of both 3 and −3.

   The _____ of a number a is denoted by $|a|$.

   Generalizations of the _____ for real numbers occur in a wide variety of mathematical settings.

   a. Area hyperbolic functions
   b. A Mathematical Theory of Communication
   c. A chemical equation
   d. Absolute value

6. In mathematics, the _____ is a test used to determine if a function is injective, surjective or bijective.

   Suppose there is a function f : X → Y with a graph., and you have a horizontal line of X x Y :
   $$y_0 \in Y, \{(x, y_0) : x \in X\} = (X \times y_0)$$

   - If the function is injective, then it can be visualized as one whose graph is never intersected by any horizontal line more than once.
   - Iff f is surjective any horizontal line will intersect the graph at least at one point
   - If f is bijective any horizontal line will intersect the graph at exactly one point.

   This test is also used to find whether or not the inverse of the function is indeed a function as well. This is due to the reflective properties of the function over y=x.

a. Disjoint sets
c. Multiset
b. Subset
d. Horizontal line test

7. In calculus, a function f defined on a subset of the real numbers with real values is called monotonic (also monotonically increasing or non-_____), if for all x and y such that x ≤ y one has f(x) ≤ f(y), so f preserves the order. In layman's terms, the sign of the slope is always positive (the curve tending upwards) or zero (i.e., non-_____, or asymptotic, or depicted as a horizontal, flat line) Likewise, a function is called monotonically _____ (non-increasing) if, whenever x ≤ y, then f(x) ≥ f(y), so it reverses the order.
   a. Decreasing
   c. Dual pair
   b. Circular convolution
   d. Tensor product of Hilbert spaces

8. In mathematics, especially in the area of abstract algebra known as ring theory, a _____ is a ring with 0 ≠ 1 such that ab = 0 implies that either a = 0 or b = 0. That is, it is a nontrivial ring without left or right zero divisors. A commutative _____ is called an integral _____.
   a. Modular representation theory
   c. Domain
   b. Left primitive ring
   d. Simple ring

9. In descriptive statistics, the _____ is the length of the smallest interval which contains all the data. It is calculated by subtracting the smallest observations from the greatest and provides an indication of statistical dispersion.

It is measured in the same units as the data.

   a. Class
   c. Kernel
   b. Bandwidth
   d. Range

10. In abstract algebra, a field extension L /K is called _____ if every element of L is _____ over K. Field extensions which are not _____.

For example, the field extension R/Q, that is the field of real numbers as an extension of the field of rational numbers, is transcendental, while the field extensions C/R and Q

   a. Identity
   c. Echo
   b. Ideal
   d. Algebraic

11. A _____ number is a positive integer which has a positive divisor other than one or itself. By definition, every integer greater than one is either a prime number or a _____ number.zero and one are considered to be neither prime nor _____. For example, the integer 14 is a _____ number because it can be factored as 2 × 7.
    a. Discontinuity
    c. Basis
    b. Key server
    d. Composite

12. In linear algebra a matrix is in _____ if

   - All nonzero rows are above any rows of all zeroes, and
   - The leading coefficient of a row is always strictly to the right of the leading coefficient of the row above it.

Chapter 5. Inverse, Exponential, and Logarithmic Functions

This is the definition used in this article, but some texts add a third condition:

- The leading coefficient of each nonzero row is one.

A matrix is in reduced _____ if it satisfies the above three conditions, and if, in addition

- Every leading coefficient is the only nonzero entry in its column.

The first non-zero entry in each row is called a pivot.

This matrix is in reduced _____:

$$\begin{bmatrix} 0 & 1 & 4 & 0 & 0 \\ 0 & 0 & 0 & 1 & 0 \\ 0 & 0 & 0 & 0 & 1 \\ 0 & 0 & 0 & 0 & 0 \end{bmatrix}.$$

The following matrix is also in _____, but not in reduced row form:

$$\begin{bmatrix} 1 & 1 & 1 & 1 \\ 0 & 9 & 0 & 2 \\ 0 & 0 & 0 & 3 \end{bmatrix}.$$

However, this matrix is not in _____, as the leading coefficient of row 3 is not strictly to the right of the leading coefficient of row 2.

$$\begin{bmatrix} 1 & 2 & 3 & 4 \\ 0 & 3 & 7 & 2 \\ 0 & 2 & 0 & 0 \end{bmatrix}$$

Every non-zero matrix can be reduced to an infinite number of echelon forms via elementary matrix transformations.

a. Row echelon form
c. Gaussian elimination

b. Portable, Extensible Toolkit for Scientific Computation
d. Reduced row echelon form

Chapter 5. Inverse, Exponential, and Logarithmic Functions

13. In mathematics, a _____ is a rectangular table of elements, which may be numbers or, more generally, any abstract quantities that can be added and multiplied. Matrices are used to describe linear equations, keep track of the coefficients of linear transformations and to record data that depend on multiple parameters. Matrices are described by the field of _____ theory.

   a. Coherent
   b. Matrix
   c. Compression
   d. Double counting

14. In mathematics and computer science, _____ (also base-16, hexa or base, of 16. It uses sixteen distinct symbols, most often the symbols 0-9 to represent values zero to nine, and A, B, C, D, E, F (or a through f) to represent values ten to fifteen.

   Its primary use is as a human friendly representation of binary coded values, so it is often used in digital electronics and computer engineering.

   a. Radix
   b. Factoradic
   c. Tetradecimal
   d. Hexadecimal

15. The _____ is a function in mathematics. The application of this function to a value x is written as ex. Equivalently, this can be written in the form e^x, where e is a mathematical constant, the base of the natural logarithm, which equals approximately 2.718281828, and is also known as Euler's number.

   a. A chemical equation
   b. Area hyperbolic functions
   c. A Mathematical Theory of Communication
   d. Exponential function

16. Exponentiation is a mathematical operation, written a^n, involving two numbers, the base a and the _____ n. When n is a positive integer, exponentiation corresponds to repeated multiplication:

$$a^n = \underbrace{a \times \cdots \times a}_{n},$$

just as multiplication by a positive integer corresponds to repeated addition:

$$a \times n = \underbrace{a + \cdots + a}_{n}.$$

The _____ is usually shown as a superscript to the right of the base. The exponentiation a^n can be read as: a raised to the n-th power, a raised to the power [of] n or possibly a raised to the _____ [of] n, or more briefly: a to the n-th power or a to the power [of] n, or even more briefly: a to the n.

   a. Exponent
   b. Exponential tree
   c. Exponentiating by squaring
   d. Exponential sum

Chapter 5. Inverse, Exponential, and Logarithmic Functions

17. _____ is the magnitude of change in the oscillating variable, with each oscillation, within an oscillating system. For instance, sound waves are oscillations in atmospheric pressure and their _____s are proportional to the change in pressure during one oscillation. If the variable undergoes regular oscillations, and a graph of the system is drawn with the oscillating variable as the vertical axis and time as the horizontal axis, the _____ is visually represented by the vertical distance between the extrema of the curve.

 a. Angular frequency
 b. Angular velocity
 c. Areal velocity
 d. Amplitude

18. A quantity is said to be subject to _____ if it decreases at a rate proportional to its value. Symbolically, this can be expressed as the following differential equation, where N is the quantity and λ is a positive number called the decay constant.

$$\frac{dN}{dt} = -\lambda N.$$

The solution to this equation is:

$$N(t) = N_0 e^{-\lambda t}.$$

Here is the quantity at time t, and $N_0 = N$ is the quantity, at time t = 0.

 a. Exponential integral
 b. Exponential formula
 c. Exponentiating by squaring
 d. Exponential decay

19. _____ is the division of one bacterium into two idential daughter cells during a process called binary fission. Hence, local doubling of the bacterial population occurs. Both daughter cells from the division do not necessarily survive.

 a. 2-3 heap
 b. Bacterial growth
 c. 120-cell
 d. 1-center problem

20. In mathematics, specifically in combinatorial commutative algebra, a convex lattice polytope P is called _____ if it has the following property: given any positive integer n, every lattice point of the dilation nP, obtained from P by scaling its vertices by the factor n and taking the convex hull of the resulting points, can be written as the sum of exactly n lattice points in P. This property plays an important role in the theory of toric varieties, where it corresponds to projective normality of the toric variety determined by P.

The simplex in R^k with the vertices at the origin and along the unit coordinate vectors is _____.

 a. Hypercube
 b. Demihypercubes
 c. Normal
 d. Polytetrahedron

21. In mathematics, the concept of a _____ tries to capture the intuitive idea of a geometrical one-dimensional and continuous object. A simple example is the circle. In everyday use of the term '_____', a straight line is not curved, but in mathematical parlance _____s include straight lines and line segments.

a. Curve
b. Quadrifolium
c. Kappa curve
d. Negative pedal curve

22. _____ is the likelihood or chance that something is the case or will happen. Theoretical _____ is used extensively in areas such as statistics, mathematics, science and philosophy to draw conclusions about the likelihood of potential events and the underlying mechanics of complex systems.

The word _____ does not have a consistent direct definition.

a. Probability
b. Statistical significance
c. Standardized moment
d. Discrete random variable

23. _____ is the concept of adding accumulated interest back to the principal, so that interest is earned on interest from that moment on. The act of declaring interest to be principal is called compounding. A loan, for example, may have its interest compounded every month: in this case, a loan with $100 principal and 1% interest per month would have a balance of $101 at the end of the first month.

a. Retained interest
b. Compound interest
c. Net interest margin securities
d. Net interest margin

24. The _____ of a quantity whose value decreases with time is the interval required for the quantity to decay to half of its initial value. The concept originated in describing how long it takes atoms to undergo radioactive decay, but also applies in a wide variety of other situations.

The term '_____' dates to 1907.

a. Half-life
b. 1-center problem
c. 120-cell
d. Radioactive decay

25. _____ is a fee, paid on borrowed capital. Assets lent include money, shares, consumer goods through hire purchase, major assets such as aircraft, and even entire factories in finance lease arrangements. The _____ is calculated upon the value of the assets in the same manner as upon money.

a. Interest
b. A Mathematical Theory of Communication
c. Interest sensitivity gap
d. Interest expense

26. _____ is the process in which an unstable atomic nucleus loses energy by emitting ionizing particles and radiation. This decay, or loss of energy, results in an atom of one type, called the parent nuclide transforming to an atom of a different type, called the daughter nuclide. For example: a carbon-14 atom emits radiation and transforms to a nitrogen-14 atom.

a. Half-life
b. Radioactive decay
c. 120-cell
d. 1-center problem

27. In mathematics and in the sciences, a _____ (plural: _____e, formulæ or _____s) is a concise way of expressing information symbolically (as in a mathematical or chemical _____), or a general relationship between quantities. One of many famous _____e is Albert Einstein's $E = mc^2$ (see special relativity

Chapter 5. Inverse, Exponential, and Logarithmic Functions

In mathematics, a _____ is a key to solve an equation with variables. For example, the problem of determining the volume of a sphere is one that requires a significant amount of integral calculus to solve.

a. 1-center problem
b. Formula
c. 2-3 heap
d. 120-cell

28. In mathematics, a _____ is a number that can be expressed as an integral of an algebraic function over an algebraic domain. Kontsevich and Zagier define a _____ as a complex number whose real and imaginary parts are values of absolutely convergent integrals of rational functions with rational coefficients, over domains in given by polynomial inequalities with rational coefficients.

a. Boussinesq approximation
b. Closeness
c. Period
d. Disk

29. In trigonometry, the _____ is a statement about a general triangle which relates the lengths of its sides to the cosine of one of its angles. Using notation as in Fig. 1, the _____ states that

$$c^2 = a^2 + b^2 - 2ab\cos(\gamma),$$

or, equivalently:

$$b^2 = c^2 + a^2 - 2ca\cos(\beta),$$
$$a^2 = b^2 + c^2 - 2bc\cos(\alpha),$$
$$\cos(\gamma) = \frac{a^2 + b^2 - c^2}{2ab}.$$

Note that c is the side opposite of angle γ, and that a and b are the two sides enclosing γ.

a. Law of cosines
b. Trigonometric functions
c. Trigonometric
d. Law of tangents

30. In physics and geometry, the _____ is the theoretical shape of a hanging flexible chain or cable when supported at its ends and acted upon by a uniform gravitational force and in equilibrium. The curve has a U shape that is similar in appearance to the parabola, though it is a different curve.

The word _____ is derived from the Latin word catena, which means 'chain'.

a. 2-3 heap
b. 120-cell
c. 1-center problem
d. Catenary

31. In mathematics, the _____ of a number to a given base is the power or exponent to which the base must be raised in order to produce the number.

Chapter 5. Inverse, Exponential, and Logarithmic Functions

For example, the _____ of 1000 to the base 10 is 3, because 3 is how many 10s one must multiply to get 1000: thus 10 × 10 × 10 = 1000; the base-2 _____ of 32 is 5 because 5 is how many 2s one must multiply to get 32: thus 2 × 2 × 2 × 2 × 2 = 32. In the language of exponents: 10^3 = 1000, so $\log_{10} 1000$ = 3, and 2^5 = 32, so $\log_2 32$ = 5.

a. Logarithm
b. 1-center problem
c. 2-3 heap
d. 120-cell

32. Any formula written in terms of logarithms may be said to be in _____.

In contexts including complex manifolds and algebraic geometry, a logarithmic differential form is a 1-form that, locally at least, can be written

$$\frac{df}{f}$$

for some meromorphic function f. That is, for some open covering, there are local representations of this differential form as a logarithmic derivative.

a. Laurent series
b. Holomorphic sheaf
c. Cauchy-Hadamard theorem
d. Logarithmic form

33. The function $\log_b(x)$ depends on both b and x, but the term _____ (or logarithmic function) in standard usage refers to a function of the form $\log_b(x)$ in which the base b is fixed and so the only argument is x. Thus there is one _____ for each value of the base b (which must be positive and must differ from 1.) Viewed in this way, the base-b _____ is the inverse function of the exponential function b^x.

a. 120-cell
b. Logarithm function
c. 1-center problem
d. 2-3 heap

34. The _____ is the logarithm with base 10. It is also known as the decadic logarithm, named after its base. It is indicated by $\log_{10}$

a. 1-center problem
b. Natural logarithm
c. Logarithmic growth
d. Common logarithm

35. The _____, formerly known as the hyperbolic logarithm, is the logarithm to the base e, where e is an irrational constant approximately equal to 2.718 281 828. It is also sometimes referred to as the Napierian logarithm, although the original meaning of this term is slightly different. In simple terms, the _____ of a number x is the power to which e would have to be raised to equal x -- for example the natural log of e itself is 1 because e^1 = e, while the _____ of 1 would be 0, since e^0 = 1.

a. Natural logarithm
b. Logarithmic growth
c. 1-center problem
d. Logarithmic identities

36. The _____ is the period of time required for a quantity to double in size or value.

Chapter 5. Inverse, Exponential, and Logarithmic Functions

a. Stretched exponential function
c. Power law
b. Zenzizenzizenzic
d. Doubling time

37. In computational complexity theory, an algorithm is said to take _____ if the asymptotic upper bound for the time it requires is proportional to the size of the input, which is usually denoted n.

Informally spoken, the running time increases linearly with the size of the input. For example, a procedure that adds up all elements of a list requires time proportional to the length of the list.

a. Linear time
c. Constructible function
b. Truth table reduction
d. Time-constructible function

38. In mathematics, a _____ is a statement that can be proved on the basis of explicitly stated or previously agreed assumptions.
a. Boolean function
c. Theorem
b. Logical value
d. Disjunction introduction

39. _____ is a term in mathematics. It can refer to:

- a _____ line, in geometry
- the trigonometric function called _____
- the _____ method, a root-finding algorithm in numerical analysis

a. Secant
c. Large set
b. Separable
d. Solvable

40. _____ is the curve along which a small object moves, under the influence of friction, when pulled on a horizontal plane by a piece of thread and a puller that moves at a right angle to the initial line between the object and the puller at an infinitesimal speed. It is therefore a curve of pursuit. It was first introduced by Claude Perrault in 1670, and later studied by Sir Isaac Newton and Christian Huygen.
a. Sinusoidal spiral
c. Cycloid
b. Folium of Descartes
d. Tractrix

41. A logistic function or _____ is the most common sigmoid curve. It models the S-curve of growth of some set P, where P might be thought of as population. The initial stage of growth is approximately exponential; then, as saturation begins, the growth slows, and at maturity, growth stops.
a. Lambert W function
c. Logarithmic integral function
b. Polylogarithm
d. Logistic curve

Chapter 6. The Trigonometric Functions

1. In geometry and trigonometry, an _____ is the figure formed by two rays sharing a common endpoint, called the vertex of the _____. The magnitude of the _____ is the 'amount of rotation' that separates the two rays, and can be measured by considering the length of circular arc swept out when one ray is rotated about the vertex to coincide with the other. Where there is no possibility of confusion, the term '_____' is used interchangeably for both the geometric configuration itself and for its angular magnitude.
   a. A chemical equation
   b. A Mathematical Theory of Communication
   c. A posteriori
   d. Angle

2. Initial objects are also called _____, and terminal objects are also called final.
   a. Terminal object
   b. Coterminal
   c. Colimit
   d. Direct limit

3. A convention universally adopted in mathematical writing is that angles given a sign are _____ if measured anticlockwise, and negative angles if measured clockwise, from a given line. If no line is specified, it can be assumed to be the x-axis in the Cartesian plane. In many geometrical situations a negative angle of −θ is effectively equivalent to a positive angle of 'one full rotation less θ'.
   a. 2-3 heap
   b. Positive angles
   c. 120-cell
   d. 1-center problem

4. A _____ consists of one quarter of the coordinate plane.
   a. Quadrant
   b. 120-cell
   c. 1-center problem
   d. 2-3 heap

5. In algebraic geometry, _____ is a notion of genericity for a set of points, or other geometric objects. It means the general case situation, as opposed to some more special or coincidental cases that are possible. Its precise meaning differs in different settings.
   a. Convexity
   b. General position
   c. Lipschitz domain
   d. Compactness measure of a shape

6. An angle equal to two right angles is called a _____ (equal to 180 degrees).
   a. Theorem
   b. Householder transformation
   c. Straight angle
   d. Loomis-Whitney inequality

7. In geometry, a _____ is a special kind of point, usually a corner of a polygon, polyhedron, or higher dimensional polytope. In the geometry of curves a _____ is a point of where the first derivative of curvature is zero. In graph theory, a _____ is the fundamental unit out of which graphs are formed
   a. Dini
   b. Crib
   c. Vertex
   d. Duality

8. In mathematics the concept of a _____ generalizes notions such as 'length', 'area', and 'volume'. Informally, given some base set, a '_____' is any consistent assignment of 'sizes' to the subsets of the base set. Depending on the application, the 'size' of a subset may be interpreted as its physical size, the amount of something that lies within the subset, or the probability that some random process will yield a result within the subset.
   a. Lattice
   b. Cusp
   c. Measure
   d. Congruent

9. The framework of quantum mechanics requires a careful definition of _____, and a thorough discussion of its practical and philosophical implications.

_____ is viewed in different ways in the many interpretations of quantum mechanics; however, despite the considerable philosophical differences, they almost universally agree on the practical question of what results from a routine quantum-physics laboratory _____. To describe this, a simple framework to use is the Copenhagen interpretation, and it will be implicitly used in this section; the utility of this approach has been verified countless times, and all other interpretations are necessarily constructed so as to give the same quantitative predictions as this in almost every case.

a. Measurement
b. Dynamic range
c. 1-center problem
d. Fundamental units

10. A _____ is an angle whose Line is the center of a circle, and whose sides pass through a pair of points on the circle, thereby subtending an arc between those two points whose angle is equal to the _____ itself. It is also known as the arc segment's angular distance.

On a sphere or ellipsoid, the _____ is delineated along a great circle.

a. Line segment
b. Hypotenuse
c. Mirror image
d. Central angle

11. A pair of angles are complementary if the sum of their measures add up to 90 degrees.

If the two _____ are adjacent (i.e. have a common vertex and share a side, but do not have any interior points in common) their non-shared sides form a right angle.

In Euclidean geometry, the two acute angles in a right triangle are complementary, because there are 180>° in a triangle and 90>° have been accounted for by the right angle.

a. Complementary angles
b. Hypotenuse
c. Conway polyhedron notation
d. Quincunx

12. The _____ is a unit of plane angle, equal to 180/π degrees, or about 57.2958 degrees. It is the standard unit of angular measurement in all areas of mathematics beyond the elementary level.

The _____ is represented by the symbol 'rad' or, more rarely, by the superscript c.

a. Radian
b. 1-center problem
c. 2-3 heap
d. 120-cell

13. In geometry and trigonometry, a _____ is defined as an angle between two straight intersecting lines of ninety degrees, or one-quarter of a circle.

a. Trigonometry
b. Sine integral
c. Trigonometric functions
d. Right angle

14. In mathematics, _____ usually refers to the direct relationship between an angle and its arc length, or for solid angle the area on a unit sphere cut out by the envelope of the vectors defining the perimeter.
    a. Quadric
    b. Geometric data analysis
    c. First Hurwitz triplet
    d. Subtended

15. A pair of angles is _____ if their measurements add up to 180 degrees. If the two _____ angles are adjacent their non-shared sides form a straight line. The supplement of 135 would be 45.
    a. Dense
    b. Supplementary
    c. Cylinder
    d. FISH

16. In mathematics, the _____ of a real number is its numerical value without regard to its sign. So, for example, 3 is the _____ of both 3 and −3.

    The _____ of a number a is denoted by $|a|$.

    Generalizations of the _____ for real numbers occur in a wide variety of mathematical settings.

    a. Area hyperbolic functions
    b. A Mathematical Theory of Communication
    c. A chemical equation
    d. Absolute value

17. An angle smaller than a right angle is called an _____ (less than 90 degrees).
    a. Euclidean geometry
    b. Ultraparallel theorem
    c. Integral geometry
    d. Acute Angle

18. A _____ is a simple shape of Euclidean geometry consisting of those points in a plane which are at a constant distance, called the radius, from a fixed point, called the center. A _____ with center A is sometimes denoted by the symbol A.

    A chord of a _____ is a line segment whose two endpoints lie on the _____.

    a. Circular segment
    b. Malfatti circles
    c. Circle
    d. Circumcircle

19. In mathematics, the _____s are analogs of the ordinary trigonometric functions. The basic _____s are the hyperbolic sine 'sinh', and the hyperbolic cosine 'cosh', from which are derived the hyperbolic tangent 'tanh', etc., in analogy to the derived trigonometric functions. The inverse _____ are the area hyperbolic sine 'arsinh' (also called 'asinh', or sometimes by the misnomer of 'arcsinh') and so on.
    a. Rectangular function
    b. Heaviside step function
    c. Square root
    d. Hyperbolic function

Chapter 6. The Trigonometric Functions

20. _____ is a quantity expressing the two-dimensional size of a defined part of a surface, typically a region bounded by a closed curve. The term surface _____ refers to the total _____ of the exposed surface of a 3-dimensional solid, such as the sum of the _____s of the exposed sides of a polyhedron. _____ is an important invariant in the differential geometry of surfaces.
   a. A Mathematical Theory of Communication
   b. Area
   c. A posteriori
   d. A chemical equation

21. A _____ or circle sector, is the portion of a circle enclosed by two radii and an arc, where the smaller area is known as the minor sector and the larger being the major sector. Its area can be calculated as described below.

Let θ be the central angle, in radians, and r the radius.

   a. Circular segment
   b. Circumcircle
   c. Circumscribed circle
   d. Circular sector

22. A _____ is one of the basic shapes of geometry: a polygon with three corners or vertices and three sides or edges which are line segments. A _____ with vertices A, B, and C is denoted ABC.

In Euclidean geometry any three non-collinear points determine a unique _____ and a unique plane.

   a. Triangle
   b. Fuhrmann circle
   c. Kepler triangle
   d. 1-center problem

23. In mathematics, the _____ functions are functions of an angle; they are important when studying triangles and modeling periodic phenomena, among many other applications.
   a. Gudermannian function
   b. Law of sines
   c. Coversine
   d. Trigonometric

24. In mathematics, the _____ are functions of an angle. They are important in the study of triangles and modeling periodic phenomena, among many other applications. _____ are commonly defined as ratios of two sides of a right triangle containing the angle, and can equivalently be defined as the lengths of various line segments from a unit circle.
   a. Law of sines
   b. Trigonometric integrals
   c. Sine
   d. Trigonometric functions

25. The mathematical concept of a _____ expresses the intuitive idea of deterministic dependence between two quantities, one of which is viewed as primary and the other as secondary. A _____ then is a way to associate a unique output for each input of a specified type, for example, a real number or an element of a given set.
   a. Grill
   b. Coherent
   c. Going up
   d. Function

26. _____ is an adjective meaning contiguous, adjoining or abutting.

In geometry, _____ is when sides meet to make an angle.

In trigonometry the _____ side of a right angled triangle is the cathetus next to the angle in question.

Chapter 6. The Trigonometric Functions

a. Adjacent
c. Ambient space
b. Ordered geometry
d. Affine geometry

27. A _____ is the longest side of a right triangle, the side opposite of the right angle. The length of the _____ of a right triangle can be found using the Pythagorean theorem, which states that the square of the length of the _____ equals the sum of the squares of the lengths of the two other sides.

For example, if one of the other sides has a length of 3 meters and the other has a length of 4 m.

a. Reflection symmetry
c. Concyclic points
b. Golden angle
d. Hypotenuse

28. In mathematics, the _____ of a number n is the number that, when added to n, yields zero. The _____ of n is denoted −n. For example, 7 is −7, because 7 + (−7) = 0, and the _____ of −0.3 is 0.3, because −0.3 + 0.3 = 0.

a. Additive inverse
c. Arity
b. Algebraic structure
d. Associativity

29. _____ is a term in mathematics. It can refer to:

- a _____ line, in geometry
- the trigonometric function called _____
- the _____ method, a root-finding algorithm in numerical analysis

a. Large set
c. Separable
b. Solvable
d. Secant

30. The _____ of an angle is the ratio of the length of the opposite side to the length of the hypotenuse. In our case

$$\sin A = \frac{\text{opposite}}{\text{hypotenuse}} = \frac{a}{h}.$$

Note that this ratio does not depend on size of the particular right triangle chosen, as long as it contains the angle A, since all such triangles are similar.

The cosine of an angle is the ratio of the length of the adjacent side to the length of the hypotenuse.

a. Right angle
c. Sine
b. Law of sines
d. Trigonometric functions

31. In trigonometry, the _____ is a function defined as $\tan x = \sin x / \cos x$. The function is so-named because it can be defined as the length of a certain segment of a _____ (in the geometric sense) to the unit circle. In plane geometry, a line is _____ to a curve, at some point, if both line and curve pass through the point with the same direction.

Chapter 6. The Trigonometric Functions

a. Tangent
c. Conformal geometry
b. Projective connection
d. Hopf conjectures

32. In mathematics, the _____ or Pythagoras' theorem is a relation in Euclidean geometry among the three sides of a right triangle. The theorem is named after the Greek mathematician Pythagoras, who by tradition is credited with its discovery and proof, although it is often argued that knowledge of the theory predates him.. The theorem is as follows:

In any right triangle, the area of the square whose side is the hypotenuse is equal to the sum of the areas of the squares whose sides are the two legs.

a. 2-3 heap
c. 120-cell
b. 1-center problem
d. Pythagorean theorem

33. In mathematics, the multiplicative inverse of a number x, denoted 1/x or x^{-1}, is the number which, when multiplied by x, yields 1. The multiplicative inverse of x is also called the _____ of x.
a. 1-center problem
c. 120-cell
b. 2-3 heap
d. Reciprocal

34. In mathematics, a _____ is a statement that can be proved on the basis of explicitly stated or previously agreed assumptions.
a. Disjunction introduction
c. Boolean function
b. Theorem
d. Logical value

35. A _____ is a device for performing mathematical calculations, distinguished from a computer by having a limited problem solving ability and an interface optimized for interactive calculation rather than programming. _____s can be hardware or software, and mechanical or electronic, and are often built into devices such as PDAs or mobile phones.

Modern electronic _____s are generally small, digital, and usually inexpensive.

a. 120-cell
c. 1-center problem
b. Calculator
d. 2-3 heap

36. In mathematics, the term _____ has several different important meanings:

- An _____ is an equality that remains true regardless of the values of any variables that appear within it, to distinguish it from an equality which is true under more particular conditions. For this, the 'triple bar' symbol ≡ is sometimes used.
- In algebra, an _____ or _____ element of a set S with a binary operation Â· is an element e that, when combined with any element x of S, produces that same x. That is, eÂ·x = xÂ·e = x for all x in S.
    o The _____ function from a set S to itself, often denoted id or id_S, s the function such that i = x for all x in S. This function serves as the _____ element in the set of all functions from S to itself with respect to function composition.
    o In linear algebra, the _____ matrix of size n is the n-by-n square matrix with ones on the main diagonal and zeros elsewhere. This matrix serves as the _____ with respect to matrix multiplication.

A common example of the first meaning is the trigonometric _____

$$\sin^2 \theta + \cos^2 \theta = 1$$

which is true for all real values of θ, as opposed to

$$\cos \theta = 1,$$

which is true only for some values of θ, not all. For example, the latter equation is true when $\theta = 0$, false when $\theta = 2$

The concepts of 'additive _____' and 'multiplicative _____' are central to the Peano axioms. The number 0 is the 'additive _____' for integers, real numbers, and complex numbers. For the real numbers, for all $a \in \mathbb{R}$,

$$0 + a = a,$$

$$a + 0 = a,\text{ and}$$

$$0 + 0 = 0.$$

Similarly, The number 1 is the 'multiplicative _____' for integers, real numbers, and complex numbers.

a. Identity
c. ARIA

b. Action
d. Intersection

37. In statistics, the _____ is the value that occurs the most frequently in a data set or a probability distribution. In some fields, notably education, sample data are often called scores, and the sample _____ is known as the modal score.

Like the statistical mean and the median, the _____ is a way of capturing important information about a random variable or a population in a single quantity.

a. Function
c. Mode

b. Field
d. Deltoid

38. In mathematics, the _____s may be described informally in several different ways. The _____s include both rational numbers, such as 42 and −23/129, and irrational numbers, such as pi and the square root of two; or, a _____ can be given by an infinite decimal representation, such as 2.4871773339...., where the digits continue in some way; or, the _____s may be thought of as points on an infinitely long number line.

These descriptions of the _____s, while intuitively accessible, are not sufficiently rigorous for the purposes of pure mathematics.

a. Minkowski distance
b. Real number
c. Pre-algebra
d. Tally marks

39. In mathematics, a _____ is a circle with a unit radius. Frequently, especially in trigonometry, 'the' _____ is the circle of radius 1 centered at the origin in the Cartesian coordinate system in the Euclidean plane. The _____ is often denoted S^1; the generalization to higher dimensions is the unit sphere.
  a. Excircle
  b. Open unit disk
  c. Inscribed angle theorem
  d. Unit circle

40. _____ is the magnitude of change in the oscillating variable, with each oscillation, within an oscillating system. For instance, sound waves are oscillations in atmospheric pressure and their _____s are proportional to the change in pressure during one oscillation. If the variable undergoes regular oscillations, and a graph of the system is drawn with the oscillating variable as the vertical axis and time as the horizontal axis, the _____ is visually represented by the vertical distance between the extrema of the curve.
  a. Amplitude
  b. Angular velocity
  c. Areal velocity
  d. Angular frequency

41. In mathematics, a _____ is a number that can be expressed as an integral of an algebraic function over an algebraic domain. Kontsevich and Zagier define a _____ as a complex number whose real and imaginary parts are values of absolutely convergent integrals of rational functions with rational coefficients, over domains in given by polynomial inequalities with rational coefficients.
  a. Closeness
  b. Disk
  c. Period
  d. Boussinesq approximation

42. In mathematics, a _____ is a function that repeats its values after some definite period has been added to its independent variable. This property is called periodicity. An illustration of a _____ with period P.

Everyday examples are seen when the variable is time; for instance the hands of a clock or the phases of the moon show periodic behaviour.

  a. Calculus controversy
  b. Method of indivisibles
  c. Hyperbolic angle
  d. Periodic function

43. In mathematics and in the sciences, a _____ (plural: _____e, formulæ or _____s) is a concise way of expressing information symbolically (as in a mathematical or chemical _____), or a general relationship between quantities. One of many famous _____e is Albert Einstein's $E = mc^2$ (see special relativity

In mathematics, a _____ is a key to solve an equation with variables. For example, the problem of determining the volume of a sphere is one that requires a significant amount of integral calculus to solve.

  a. 2-3 heap
  b. 120-cell
  c. Formula
  d. 1-center problem

44. The _____ or sinusoid is a function that occurs often in mathematics, physics, signal processing, audition, electrical engineering, and many other fields. Its most basic form is:

$$y(t) = A \cdot \sin(\omega t + \theta)$$

which describes a wavelike function of time with:

- peak deviation from center = A
- angular frequency ω,
- phase = θ
    - When the phase is non-zero, the entire waveform appears to be shifted in time by the amount θ/ω seconds. A negative value represents a delay, and a positive value represents a 'head-start'.

The _____ is important in physics because it retains its waveshape when added to another _____ of the same frequency and arbitrary phase. It is the only periodic waveform that has this property. This property leads to its importance in Fourier analysis and makes it acoustically unique.

a. Trigonometric functions
c. Sine wave
b. Law of sines
d. Law of tangents

45. In mathematics and computer science, _____ (also base-16, hexa or base, of 16. It uses sixteen distinct symbols, most often the symbols 0-9 to represent values zero to nine, and A, B, C, D, E, F (or a through f) to represent values ten to fifteen.

Its primary use is as a human friendly representation of binary coded values, so it is often used in digital electronics and computer engineering.

a. Factoradic
c. Radix
b. Hexadecimal
d. Tetradecimal

46. The _____ , is achieved in a packed stadium when successive groups of spectators briefly stand and raise their arms. Each spectator is required to rise at the same time as those straight in front and behind, and slightly after the person immediately to either the right or the left. Immediately upon stretching to full height, the spectator returns to the usual seated position.

a. Lagrangian
c. Pauli exclusion principle
b. Wave
d. Thermodynamic limit

47. A branch or tree branch (sometimes referred to in botany as a ramus) is a woody structural member connected to but not part of the central trunk of a tree (or sometimes a shrub.) Large _____ are known as boughs and small _____ are known as twigs.

While _____ can be nearly horizontal, vertical, or diagonal, the majority of trees have upwardly diagonal _____ .

a. 2-3 heap
c. Branches
b. 120-cell
d. 1-center problem

Chapter 6. The Trigonometric Functions

48. The _____ is the distance between a point and an axis in the Cartesian Coordinate System.
   a. 2-3 heap
   b. 1-center problem
   c. 120-cell
   d. Y-coordinate

49. An _____ of a real-valued function y = f(x) is a curve which describes the behavior of f as either x or y tends to infinity.

In other words, as one moves along the graph of f(x) in some direction, the distance between it and the _____ eventually becomes smaller than any distance that one may specify.

If a curve A has the curve B as an _____, one says that A is asymptotic to B. Similarly B is asymptotic to A, so A and B are called asymptotic.

   a. Isoperimetric dimension
   b. Improper integral
   c. Infinite product
   d. Asymptote

50. In mathematics, especially in the area of abstract algebra known as ring theory, a _____ is a ring with 0 ≠ 1 such that ab = 0 implies that either a = 0 or b = 0. That is, it is a nontrivial ring without left or right zero divisors. A commutative _____ is called an integral _____.
   a. Modular representation theory
   b. Simple ring
   c. Left primitive ring
   d. Domain

51. In descriptive statistics, the _____ is the length of the smallest interval which contains all the data. It is calculated by subtracting the smallest observations from the greatest and provides an indication of statistical dispersion.

It is measured in the same units as the data.

   a. Bandwidth
   b. Class
   c. Range
   d. Kernel

52. In abstract algebra, a field extension L /K is called _____ if every element of L is _____ over K. Field extensions which are not _____.

For example, the field extension R/Q, that is the field of real numbers as an extension of the field of rational numbers, is transcendental, while the field extensions C/R and Q

   a. Ideal
   b. Identity
   c. Echo
   d. Algebraic

Chapter 6. The Trigonometric Functions

53. In mathematics, an _____ is a statement about the relative size or order of two objects, or about whether they are the same or not

- The notation a < b means that a is less than b.
- The notation a > b means that a is greater than b.
- The notation a ≠ b means that a is not equal to b, but does not say that one is bigger than the other or even that they can be compared in size.

In all these cases, a is not equal to b, hence, '_____'.

These relations are known as strict _____

- The notation a ≤ b means that a is less than or equal to b;
- The notation a ≥ b means that a is greater than or equal to b;

An additional use of the notation is to show that one quantity is much greater than another, normally by several orders of magnitude.

- The notation a << b means that a is much less than b.
- The notation a >> b means that a is much greater than b.

If the sense of the _____ is the same for all values of the variables for which its members are defined, then the _____ is called an 'absolute' or 'unconditional' _____. If the sense of an _____ holds only for certain values of the variables involved, but is reversed or destroyed for other values of the variables, it is called a conditional _____.

An _____ may appear unsolvable because it only states whether a number is larger or smaller than another number; but it is possible to apply the same operations for equalities to inequalities. For example, to find x for the _____ 10x > 23 one would divide 23 by 10.

 a. A Mathematical Theory of Communication
 c. A posteriori
 b. Inequality
 d. A chemical equation

54. In mathematics, the _____ or cyclometric functions are the so-called inverse functions of the trigonometric functions, though they do not meet the official definition for inverse functions as their domains are subsets of the images of the original functions.

 a. A posteriori
 c. A chemical equation
 b. A Mathematical Theory of Communication
 d. Inverse trigonometric functions

55. In mathematics, the _____s are an extension of the real numbers obtained by adjoining an imaginary unit, denoted i, which satisfies:

$$i^2 = -1.$$

Chapter 6. The Trigonometric Functions

Every _____ can be written in the form a + bi, where a and b are real numbers called the real part and the imaginary part of the _____, respectively.

_____s are a field, and thus have addition, subtraction, multiplication, and division operations. These operations extend the corresponding operations on real numbers, although with a number of additional elegant and useful properties, e.g., negative real numbers can be obtained by squaring _____s.

- a. Complex number
- b. 1-center problem
- c. Real part
- d. 120-cell

56. In mathematics, an arithmetic progression or _____ is a sequence of numbers such that the difference of any two successive members of the sequence is a constant. For instance, the sequence 3, 5, 7, 9, 11, 13... is an arithmetic progression with common difference 2.
- a. Edgeworth series
- b. Alternating series test
- c. Eisenstein series
- d. Arithmetic sequence

57. _____ is a branch of mathematics which focuses on the study of matrices. Initially a sub-branch of linear algebra, it has grown to cover subjects related to graph theory, algebra, combinatorics, and statistics as well.

The term matrix was first coined in 1848 by J.J. Sylvester as a name of an array of numbers.

- a. Pairing
- b. Matrix theory
- c. Semi-simple operators
- d. Segre classification

58. _____ is any effect, either deliberately engendered or inherent to a system, that tends to reduce the amplitude of oscillations of an oscillatory system.

In physics and engineering, _____ may be mathematically modelled as a force synchronous with the velocity of the object but opposite in direction to it. If such force is also proportional to the velocity, as for a simple mechanical viscous damper, the force F may be related to the velocity v by

$$\mathbf{F} = -c\mathbf{v}$$

where c is the viscous _____ coefficient, given in units of newton-seconds per meter.

- a. 120-cell
- b. Vibrating string
- c. 1-center problem
- d. Damping

59. _____ is a branch of mathematics that deals with triangles, particularly those plane triangles in which one angle has 90 degrees. _____ deals with relationships between the sides and the angles of triangles and with the trigonometric functions, which describe those relationships.

_____ has applications in both pure mathematics and in applied mathematics, where it is essential in many branches of science and technology.

a. Trigonometric functions
c. Sine
b. Law of sines
d. Trigonometry

60. The Q-TIP of a geographic location is its height above a fixed reference point, often the mean sea level. _____, or geometric height, is mainly used when referring to points on the Earth's surface, while altitude or geopotential height is used for points above the surface, such as an aircraft in flight or a spacecraft in orbit.

Less commonly, _____ is measured using the center of the Earth as the reference point.

a. Elevation
c. A posteriori
b. A Mathematical Theory of Communication
d. A chemical equation

61. In acoustics and telecommunication, the _____ of a wave is a component frequency of the signal that is an integer multiple of the fundamental frequency. For example, if the frequency is f, the _____s have frequency 2f, 3f, 4f, etc, as well as f itself. The _____s have the property that they are all periodic at the signal frequency.

a. Harmonic
c. Robinson-Dadson curves
b. Digital room correction
d. Subharmonic

62. In abstract algebra, a module S over a ring R is called _____ or irreducible if it is not the zero module 0 and if its only submodules are 0 and S. Understanding the _____ modules over a ring is usually helpful because these modules form the 'building blocks' of all other modules in a certain sense.

Abelian groups are the same as Z-modules.

a. Basis
c. Harmonic series
b. Derivation
d. Simple

63. _____ is the motion of a simple harmonic oscillator, a motion that is neither driven nor damped. The motion is periodic, as it repeats itself at standard intervals in a specific manner - described as being sinusoidal, with constant amplitude. It is characterized by its amplitude, its period which is the time for a single oscillation, its frequency which is the number of cycles per unit time, and its phase, which determines the starting point on the sine wave.

a. Stretch rule
c. Kinematics
b. Simple harmonic motion
d. Configuration space

64. In statistics the _____ of an event i is the number n_i of times the event occurred in the experiment or the study. These frequencies are often graphically represented in histograms.

We speak of absolute frequencies, when the counts n_i themselves are given and of

$$f_i = \frac{n_i}{N} = \frac{n_i}{\sum_i n_i}$$

Taking the f_i for all i and tabulating or plotting them leads to a _____ distribution.

a. Robinson-Dadson curves
c. Subharmonic
b. Digital room correction
d. Frequency

65. In mathematics, _____ is the behaviour of a sequence of real numbers or a real-valued function, which does not converge, but also does not diverge to +∞ or -∞; that is, _____ is the failure to have a limit, and is also a quantitative measure for that.

_____ is defined as the difference between the limit superior and limit inferior. It is undefined if both are +∞ or both are -∞.

a. A Mathematical Theory of Communication
c. A posteriori
b. A chemical equation
d. Oscillation

Chapter 7. Analytic Trigonometry

1. In mathematics, the _____ functions are functions of an angle; they are important when studying triangles and modeling periodic phenomena, among many other applications.
   a. Law of sines
   b. Gudermannian function
   c. Coversine
   d. Trigonometric

2. In mathematics, _____ are equalities that involve trigonometric functions that are true for every single value of the occurring variables. These identities are useful whenever expressions involving trigonometric functions need to be simplified. An important application is the integration of non-trigonometric functions: a common trick involves first using the substitution rule with a trigonometric function, and then simplifying the resulting integral with a trigonometric identity.
   a. Trigonometric identities
   b. 2-3 heap
   c. 1-center problem
   d. 120-cell

3. The mathematical concept of a _____ expresses the intuitive idea of deterministic dependence between two quantities, one of which is viewed as primary and the other as secondary. A _____ then is a way to associate a unique output for each input of a specified type, for example, a real number or an element of a given set.
   a. Going up
   b. Coherent
   c. Grill
   d. Function

4. The _____ is a unit of plane angle, equal to 180/π degrees, or about 57.2958 degrees. It is the standard unit of angular measurement in all areas of mathematics beyond the elementary level.

   The _____ is represented by the symbol 'rad' or, more rarely, by the superscript c.

   a. Radian
   b. 1-center problem
   c. 2-3 heap
   d. 120-cell

5. The _____ of an angle is the ratio of the length of the opposite side to the length of the hypotenuse. In our case

   $$\sin A = \frac{\text{opposite}}{\text{hypotenuse}} = \frac{a}{h}.$$

   Note that this ratio does not depend on size of the particular right triangle chosen, as long as it contains the angle A, since all such triangles are similar.

   The cosine of an angle is the ratio of the length of the adjacent side to the length of the hypotenuse.

   a. Law of sines
   b. Trigonometric functions
   c. Right angle
   d. Sine

6. In mathematics, the _____ of a real number is its numerical value without regard to its sign. So, for example, 3 is the _____ of both 3 and −3.

   The _____ of a number a is denoted by $|a|$.

   Generalizations of the _____ for real numbers occur in a wide variety of mathematical settings.

a. A Mathematical Theory of Communication
b. Area hyperbolic functions
c. Absolute value
d. A chemical equation

7. In mathematics, the _____ are functions of an angle. They are important in the study of triangles and modeling periodic phenomena, among many other applications. _____ are commonly defined as ratios of two sides of a right triangle containing the angle, and can equivalently be defined as the lengths of various line segments from a unit circle.
a. Trigonometric integrals
b. Sine
c. Law of sines
d. Trigonometric functions

8. In trigonometry, the _____ is a function defined as tan x = $^{\sin x}/_{\cos x}$. The function is so-named because it can be defined as the length of a certain segment of a _____ (in the geometric sense) to the unit circle. In plane geometry, a line is _____ to a curve, at some point, if both line and curve pass through the point with the same direction.
a. Hopf conjectures
b. Projective connection
c. Conformal geometry
d. Tangent

9. In mathematics, a _____ is a circle with a unit radius. Frequently, especially in trigonometry, 'the' _____ is the circle of radius 1 centered at the origin in the Cartesian coordinate system in the Euclidean plane. The _____ is often denoted S^1; the generalization to higher dimensions is the unit sphere.
a. Open unit disk
b. Excircle
c. Unit circle
d. Inscribed angle theorem

10. A _____ is a simple shape of Euclidean geometry consisting of those points in a plane which are at a constant distance, called the radius, from a fixed point, called the center. A _____ with center A is sometimes denoted by the symbol A.

A chord of a _____ is a line segment whose two endpoints lie on the _____.

a. Malfatti circles
b. Circle
c. Circumcircle
d. Circular segment

11. In mathematics, a _____ is a polynomial equation of the second degree. The general form is

$$ax^2 + bx + c = 0,$$

where a ≠ 0.

The letters a, b, and c are called coefficients: the quadratic coefficient a is the coefficient of x^2, the linear coefficient b is the coefficient of x, and c is the constant coefficient, also called the free term or constant term.

a. Quartic equation
b. Difference of two squares
c. Quadratic equation
d. Linear equation

12. In mathematics, a _____ is a statement that can be proved on the basis of explicitly stated or previously agreed assumptions.

a. Boolean function
c. Logical value
b. Disjunction introduction
d. Theorem

13. A _____ is a device for performing mathematical calculations, distinguished from a computer by having a limited problem solving ability and an interface optimized for interactive calculation rather than programming. _____s can be hardware or software, and mechanical or electronic, and are often built into devices such as PDAs or mobile phones.

Modern electronic _____s are generally small, digital, and usually inexpensive.

a. 2-3 heap
c. 1-center problem
b. 120-cell
d. Calculator

14. In mathematics and in the sciences, a _____ (plural: _____e, formulæ or _____s) is a concise way of expressing information symbolically (as in a mathematical or chemical _____), or a general relationship between quantities. One of many famous _____e is Albert Einstein's E = mc² (see special relativity

In mathematics, a _____ is a key to solve an equation with variables. For example, the problem of determining the volume of a sphere is one that requires a significant amount of integral calculus to solve.

a. 120-cell
c. 2-3 heap
b. 1-center problem
d. Formula

15. In mathematics, the term _____ has several different important meanings:

- An _____ is an equality that remains true regardless of the values of any variables that appear within it, to distinguish it from an equality which is true under more particular conditions. For this, the 'triple bar' symbol ≡ is sometimes used.
- In algebra, an _____ or _____ element of a set S with a binary operation Â· is an element e that, when combined with any element x of S, produces that same x. That is, eÂ·x = xÂ·e = x for all x in S.
    - The _____ function from a set S to itself, often denoted id or id$_S$, s the function such that i = x for all x in S. This function serves as the _____ element in the set of all functions from S to itself with respect to function composition.
    - In linear algebra, the _____ matrix of size n is the n-by-n square matrix with ones on the main diagonal and zeros elsewhere. This matrix serves as the _____ with respect to matrix multiplication.

A common example of the first meaning is the trigonometric _____

$$\sin^2 \theta + \cos^2 \theta = 1$$

which is true for all real values of θ, as opposed to

$$\cos \theta = 1,$$

which is true only for some values of θ, not all. For example, the latter equation is true when $\theta = 0$, false when $\theta = 2$

Chapter 7. Analytic Trigonometry

The concepts of 'additive _____' and 'multiplicative _____' are central to the Peano axioms. The number 0 is the 'additive _____' for integers, real numbers, and complex numbers. For the real numbers, for all $a \in \mathbb{R}$,

$$0 + a = a,$$

$$a + 0 = a, \text{ and}$$

$$0 + 0 = 0.$$

Similarly, The number 1 is the 'multiplicative _____' for integers, real numbers, and complex numbers.

a. Action
b. Intersection
c. ARIA
d. Identity

16. In mathematics, a function f is _____ of a function g if f whenever A and B are complementary angles. This definition typically applies to trigonometric functions.
    a. Birkhoff interpolation
    b. Balian-Low theorem
    c. Boxcar function
    d. Cofunction

17. In mathematics, an arithmetic progression or _____ is a sequence of numbers such that the difference of any two successive members of the sequence is a constant. For instance, the sequence 3, 5, 7, 9, 11, 13... is an arithmetic progression with common difference 2.
    a. Edgeworth series
    b. Alternating series test
    c. Eisenstein series
    d. Arithmetic sequence

18. _____ is a quantity expressing the two-dimensional size of a defined part of a surface, typically a region bounded by a closed curve. The term surface _____ refers to the total _____ of the exposed surface of a 3-dimensional solid, such as the sum of the _____s of the exposed sides of a polyhedron. _____ is an important invariant in the differential geometry of surfaces.
    a. A Mathematical Theory of Communication
    b. Area
    c. A posteriori
    d. A chemical equation

19. A _____ is one of the basic shapes of geometry: a polygon with three corners or vertices and three sides or edges which are line segments. A _____ with vertices A, B, and C is denoted ABC.

In Euclidean geometry any three non-collinear points determine a unique _____ and a unique plane.

a. Kepler triangle
b. Triangle
c. 1-center problem
d. Fuhrmann circle

20. _____ is the magnitude of change in the oscillating variable, with each oscillation, within an oscillating system. For instance, sound waves are oscillations in atmospheric pressure and their _____s are proportional to the change in pressure during one oscillation. If the variable undergoes regular oscillations, and a graph of the system is drawn with the oscillating variable as the vertical axis and time as the horizontal axis, the _____ is visually represented by the vertical distance between the extrema of the curve.

a. Areal velocity
b. Angular frequency
c. Angular velocity
d. Amplitude

21. In mathematics, the _____s are analogs of the ordinary trigonometric functions. The basic _____s are the hyperbolic sine 'sinh', and the hyperbolic cosine 'cosh', from which are derived the hyperbolic tangent 'tanh', etc., in analogy to the derived trigonometric functions. The inverse _____ are the area hyperbolic sine 'arsinh' (also called 'asinh', or sometimes by the misnomer of 'arcsinh') and so on.

a. Heaviside step function
b. Square root
c. Rectangular function
d. Hyperbolic function

22. A _____ or circle sector, is the portion of a circle enclosed by two radii and an arc, where the smaller area is known as the minor sector and the larger being the major sector. Its area can be calculated as described below.

Let θ be the central angle, in radians, and r the radius.

a. Circumcircle
b. Circular segment
c. Circumscribed circle
d. Circular sector

23. _____ is a core concept of basic mathematics, specifically in the fields of infinitesimal calculus and mathematical analysis. Given a function f

$$\int_a^b f(x)\, dx,$$

is equal to the area of a region in the xy-plane bounded by the graph of f, the x-axis, and the vertical lines x = a and x = b, with areas below the x-axis being subtracted.

The term 'integral' may also refer to the notion of antiderivative, a function F whose derivative is the given function f.

a. OMAC
b. Epigraph
c. Apex
d. Integration

24. In mathematics, the _____ of a number n is the number that, when added to n, yields zero. The _____ of n is denoted −n. For example, 7 is −7, because 7 + (−7) = 0, and the _____ of −0.3 is 0.3, because −0.3 + 0.3 = 0.

a. Algebraic structure
b. Arity
c. Associativity
d. Additive inverse

Chapter 7. Analytic Trigonometry

25. In mathematics, the _____ or cyclometric functions are the so-called inverse functions of the trigonometric functions, though they do not meet the official definition for inverse functions as their domains are subsets of the images of the original functions.
    a. A posteriori
    b. A Mathematical Theory of Communication
    c. A chemical equation
    d. Inverse trigonometric functions

26. Determining _____ was historically difficult. Although many methods were used for specific curves, the advent of calculus led to a general formula that provides closed-form solutions in some cases.

    A curve in, say, the plane can be approximated by connecting a finite number of points on the curve using line segments to create a polygonal path.

    a. Antidifferentiation
    b. Indefinite integral
    c. Integral
    d. Arc length

27. An _____ of a real-valued function y = f(x) is a curve which describes the behavior of f as either x or y tends to infinity.

    In other words, as one moves along the graph of f(x) in some direction, the distance between it and the _____ eventually becomes smaller than any distance that one may specify.

    If a curve A has the curve B as an _____, one says that A is asymptotic to B. Similarly B is asymptotic to A, so A and B are called asymptotic.

    a. Improper integral
    b. Isoperimetric dimension
    c. Infinite product
    d. Asymptote

28. In mathematics, the _____ or Pythagoras' theorem is a relation in Euclidean geometry among the three sides of a right triangle. The theorem is named after the Greek mathematician Pythagoras, who by tradition is credited with its discovery and proof, although it is often argued that knowledge of the theory predates him.. The theorem is as follows:

    In any right triangle, the area of the square whose side is the hypotenuse is equal to the sum of the areas of the squares whose sides are the two legs.

    a. Pythagorean theorem
    b. 2-3 heap
    c. 1-center problem
    d. 120-cell

Chapter 8. Applications of Trigonometry

1. In trigonometry, the _____ is a statement about a general triangle which relates the lengths of its sides to the cosine of one of its angles. Using notation as in Fig. 1, the _____ states that

$$c^2 = a^2 + b^2 - 2ab\cos(\gamma),$$

or, equivalently:

$$b^2 = c^2 + a^2 - 2ca\cos(\beta),$$
$$a^2 = b^2 + c^2 - 2bc\cos(\alpha),$$
$$\cos(\gamma) = \frac{a^2 + b^2 - c^2}{2ab}.$$

Note that c is the side opposite of angle γ, and that a and b are the two sides enclosing γ.

   a. Law of cosines
   b. Trigonometric
   c. Trigonometric functions
   d. Law of tangents

2. A _____ is one of the basic shapes of geometry: a polygon with three corners or vertices and three sides or edges which are line segments. A _____ with vertices A, B, and C is denoted ABC.

In Euclidean geometry any three non-collinear points determine a unique _____ and a unique plane.

   a. Kepler triangle
   b. 1-center problem
   c. Fuhrmann circle
   d. Triangle

3. The _____ of an angle is the ratio of the length of the opposite side to the length of the hypotenuse. In our case

$$\sin A = \frac{\text{opposite}}{\text{hypotenuse}} = \frac{a}{h}.$$

Note that this ratio does not depend on size of the particular right triangle chosen, as long as it contains the angle A, since all such triangles are similar.

The cosine of an angle is the ratio of the length of the adjacent side to the length of the hypotenuse.

   a. Right angle
   b. Trigonometric functions
   c. Sine
   d. Law of sines

4. In geometry and trigonometry, an _____ is the figure formed by two rays sharing a common endpoint, called the vertex of the _____. The magnitude of the _____ is the 'amount of rotation' that separates the two rays, and can be measured by considering the length of circular arc swept out when one ray is rotated about the vertex to coincide with the other. Where there is no possibility of confusion, the term '_____' is used interchangeably for both the geometric configuration itself and for its angular magnitude.

a. Angle	b. A chemical equation
c. A posteriori	d. A Mathematical Theory of Communication

5. The Q-TIP of a geographic location is its height above a fixed reference point, often the mean sea level. _____, or geometric height, is mainly used when referring to points on the Earth's surface, while altitude or geopotential height is used for points above the surface, such as an aircraft in flight or a spacecraft in orbit.

Less commonly, _____ is measured using the center of the Earth as the reference point.

a. Elevation	b. A posteriori
c. A chemical equation	d. A Mathematical Theory of Communication

6. In geometry, a _____ is a quadrilateral with two sets of parallel sides. The opposite sides of a _____ are of equal length, and the opposite angles of a _____ are congruent. The three-dimensional counterpart of a _____ is a parallelepiped.

a. 120-cell	b. 2-3 heap
c. 1-center problem	d. Parallelogram

7. _____ is a quantity expressing the two-dimensional size of a defined part of a surface, typically a region bounded by a closed curve. The term surface _____ refers to the total _____ of the exposed surface of a 3-dimensional solid, such as the sum of the _____s of the exposed sides of a polyhedron. _____ is an important invariant in the differential geometry of surfaces.

a. Area	b. A posteriori
c. A Mathematical Theory of Communication	d. A chemical equation

8. In mathematics, the _____s are analogs of the ordinary trigonometric functions. The basic _____s are the hyperbolic sine 'sinh', and the hyperbolic cosine 'cosh', from which are derived the hyperbolic tangent 'tanh', etc., in analogy to the derived trigonometric functions. The inverse _____ are the area hyperbolic sine 'arsinh' (also called 'asinh', or sometimes by the misnomer of 'arcsinh') and so on.

a. Rectangular function	b. Heaviside step function
c. Square root	d. Hyperbolic function

9. A _____ or circle sector, is the portion of a circle enclosed by two radii and an arc, where the smaller area is known as the minor sector and the larger being the major sector. Its area can be calculated as described below.

Let θ be the central angle, in radians, and r the radius.

a. Circumcircle	b. Circular segment
c. Circular sector	d. Circumscribed circle

10. In mathematics and in the sciences, a _____ (plural: _____e, formulæ or _____s) is a concise way of expressing information symbolically (as in a mathematical or chemical _____), or a general relationship between quantities. One of many famous _____e is Albert Einstein's $E = mc^2$ (see special relativity

In mathematics, a _____ is a key to solve an equation with variables. For example, the problem of determining the volume of a sphere is one that requires a significant amount of integral calculus to solve.

a. 1-center problem
b. 120-cell
c. 2-3 heap
d. Formula

11. In the study of metric spaces in mathematics, there are various notions of two metrics on the same underlying space being 'the same', or _____.

In the following, M will denote a non-empty set and d_1 and d_2 will denote two metrics on M.

The two metrics d_1 and d_2 are said to be topologically _____ if they generate the same topology on M.

a. A chemical equation
b. A posteriori
c. A Mathematical Theory of Communication
d. Equivalent

12. Initial objects are also called _____, and terminal objects are also called final.
a. Colimit
b. Direct limit
c. Terminal object
d. Coterminal

13. In physics and in _____ calculus, a _____ is a concept characterized by a magnitude and a direction. A _____ can be thought of as an arrow in Euclidean space, drawn from an initial point A pointing to a terminal point B.
a. Deviation
b. Dominance
c. Vector
d. Constraint

14. In geometry, a _____ is a part of a line that is bounded by two distinct end points, and contains every point on the line between its end points. Examples of _____s include the sides of a triangle or square. More generally, when the end points are both vertices of a polygon, the _____ is either an edge if they are adjacent vertices, or otherwise a diagonal.
a. Golden angle
b. Line segment
c. Cuboid
d. Transversal line

15. In mathematics, _____ is one of the basic operations defining a vector space in linear algebra. Note that _____ is different from scalar product which is an inner product between two vectors.

More specifically, if K is a field and V is a vector space over K, then _____ is a function from K × V to V.

a. Frobenius normal form
b. Jordan normal form
c. Non-negative matrix factorization
d. Scalar multiplication

16. _____ of an object is its speed in a particular direction.
a. Velocity
b. Discontinuity
c. Rolle's Theorem
d. Maxima

17. In mathematics, an arithmetic progression or _____ is a sequence of numbers such that the difference of any two successive members of the sequence is a constant. For instance, the sequence 3, 5, 7, 9, 11, 13... is an arithmetic progression with common difference 2.

a. Edgeworth series
b. Eisenstein series
c. Alternating series test
d. Arithmetic sequence

18. In mathematics, the simplest form of the _____ belongs to elementary geometry. It states that the sum of the squares of the lengths of the four sides of a parallelogram equals the sum of the squares of the lengths of the two diagonals. With the notation in the diagram on the right, this can be stated as

$$(AB)^2 + (BC)^2 + (CD)^2 + (DA)^2 = (AC)^2 + (BD)^2.$$

In case the parallelogram is a rectangle, the two diagonals are of equal lengths and the statement reduces to the Pythagorean theorem.

a. Parallelogram law
b. Square lattice
c. Half-space
d. Homothetic center

19. A _____ is a vector which represents the position of an object in space in relation to an arbitrary reference point. The concept applies to two- or three-dimensional space. The term is also used as a means of deriving displacement by the spatial comparison of two or more _____s and are usually 2- or, through hyperspace-based theories, 3-dimensional or N-dimensional if belonging to an N-dimensional Euclidean hyperspace.

a. Generalized Morse sequence
b. Radius vector
c. Minimum distance
d. Position vector

20. In mathematics, the _____ of a real number is its numerical value without regard to its sign. So, for example, 3 is the _____ of both 3 and −3.

The _____ of a number a is denoted by $|a|$.

Generalizations of the _____ for real numbers occur in a wide variety of mathematical settings.

a. A Mathematical Theory of Communication
b. A chemical equation
c. Area hyperbolic functions
d. Absolute value

21. _____ is a branch of mathematics which focuses on the study of matrices. Initially a sub-branch of linear algebra, it has grown to cover subjects related to graph theory, algebra, combinatorics, and statistics as well.

The term matrix was first coined in 1848 by J.J. Sylvester as a name of an array of numbers.

a. Semi-simple operators
b. Segre classification
c. Pairing
d. Matrix theory

22. In mathematics, _____ are a concept central to linear algebra and related fields of mathematics

Suppose that K is a field and V is a vector space over K.

a. Polarization
b. Linear span
c. Setoid
d. Linear combinations

23. In combinatorial mathematics, a _____ is an un-ordered collection of distinct elements, usually of a prescribed size and taken from a given set. Given such a set S, a _____ of elements of S is just a subset of S, where as always forsets the order of the elements is not taken into account. Also, as always forsets, no elements can be repeated more than once in a _____; this is often referred to as a 'collection without repetition'.

a. Heawood number
b. Fill-in
c. Combination
d. Sparsity

24. In mathematics, the _____ is an operation which takes two vectors over the real numbers R and returns a real-valued scalar quantity. It is the standard inner product of the orthonormal Euclidean space.

The _____ of two vectors a = [a_1, a_2, …, a_n] and b = [b_1, b_2, …, b_n] is defined as:

$$\mathbf{a} \cdot \mathbf{b} = \sum_{i=1}^{n} a_i b_i = a_1 b_1 + a_2 b_2 + \cdots + a_n b_n$$

where Σ denotes summation notation and n is the dimension of the vectors.

a. Principal axis theorem
b. Dot product
c. Matrix determinant lemma
d. Conjugate transpose

25. In mathematics, an _____ is a vector space with the additional structure of inner product. This additional structure associates each pair of vectors in the space with a scalar quantity known as the inner product of the vectors. Inner products allow the rigorous introduction of intuitive geometrical notions such as the length of a vector or the angle between two vectors.

a. A Mathematical Theory of Communication
b. Inner product space
c. A posteriori
d. A chemical equation

26. In mathematics, two vectors are _____ if they are perpendicular. For example, a subway and the street above, although they do not physically intersect, are _____ if they cross at a right angle.

a. Algebraic structure
b. Orthogonal
c. Unique factorization domain
d. Additive identity

27. A _____ of a curve is the envelope of a family of congruent circles centered on the curve. It generalises the concept of _____ lines.

It is sometimes called the offset curve but the term 'offset' often refers also to translation.

a. Cissoid
b. Parallel
c. Cycloid
d. Bifolium

Chapter 8. Applications of Trigonometry

28. In mathematics, a _____ is a statement that can be proved on the basis of explicitly stated or previously agreed assumptions.
    a. Disjunction introduction
    b. Logical value
    c. Boolean function
    d. Theorem

29. _____ is the magnitude of change in the oscillating variable, with each oscillation, within an oscillating system. For instance, sound waves are oscillations in atmospheric pressure and their _____s are proportional to the change in pressure during one oscillation. If the variable undergoes regular oscillations, and a graph of the system is drawn with the oscillating variable as the vertical axis and time as the horizontal axis, the _____ is visually represented by the vertical distance between the extrema of the curve.
    a. Angular velocity
    b. Amplitude
    c. Areal velocity
    d. Angular frequency

30. In mathematics, a _____ is a number that can be expressed as an integral of an algebraic function over an algebraic domain. Kontsevich and Zagier define a _____ as a complex number whose real and imaginary parts are values of absolutely convergent integrals of rational functions with rational coefficients, over domains in given by polynomial inequalities with rational coefficients.
    a. Period
    b. Disk
    c. Boussinesq approximation
    d. Closeness

31. In linear algebra and functional analysis, a _____ is a linear transformation P from a vector space to itself such that $P^2 = P$. It leaves its image unchanged. Though abstract, this definition of '_____' formalizes and generalizes the idea of graphical _____.
    a. Deviance
    b. Characteristic function
    c. Critical point
    d. Projection

32. The _____ is the derived unit of energy in the International System of Units. It is defined as:

$$1\,\text{J} = 1\,\text{kg} \cdot \frac{\text{m}^2}{\text{s}^2}$$

One _____ is the amount of energy required to perform the following actions:

- The work done by a force of one newton travelling through a distance of one meter;
- The work required to move an electric charge of one coulomb through an electrical potential difference of one volt; or one coulomb volt, with the symbol CÂ·V;
- The work done to produce power of one watt continuously for one second; or one watt second, with the symbol WÂ·s. Thus a kilowatt hour is 3,600,000 _____s or 3.6 megajoules;
- The kinetic energy of a 2 kg mass moving at a velocity of 1 m/s. The energy is linear in the mass but quadratic in the velocity, being given by E = 1/2mv^2;

   a. 1-center problem
   b. 120-cell
   c. 2-3 heap
   d. Joule

33. The _____ (symbol: N) is the SI derived unit of force, named after Isaac _____ in recognition of his work on classical mechanics.

Chapter 8. Applications of Trigonometry

The _____ is the unit of force derived in the SI system; it is equal to the amount of force required to accelerate a mass of one kilogram at a rate of one meter per second per second. Algebraically:

$$1\text{ N} = 1\ \frac{\text{kg} \cdot \text{m}}{\text{s}^2}.$$

- 1 N is the force of Earth's gravity on an object with a mass of about 102 g ($\frac{1}{9.8}$ kg) (such as a small apple.)
- On Earth's surface, a mass of 1 kg exerts a force of approximately 9.80665 N [down] (or 1 kgf.) The approximation of 1 kg corresponding to 10 N is sometimes used as a rule of thumb in everyday life and in engineering.
- The force of Earth's gravity on a human being with a mass of 70 kg is approximately 687 N.
- The dot product of force and distance is mechanical work. Thus, in SI units, a force of 1 N exerted over a distance of 1 m is 1 NÂ·m of work. The Work-Energy Theorem states that the work done on a body is equal to the change in energy of the body. 1 NÂ·m = 1 J (joule), the SI unit of energy.
- It is common to see forces expressed in kilonewtons or kN, where 1 kN = 1 000 N.

a. 1-center problem
b. 120-cell
c. 2-3 heap
d. Newton

34. In mathematics, the _____s are an extension of the real numbers obtained by adjoining an imaginary unit, denoted i, which satisfies:

$$i^2 = -1.$$

Every _____ can be written in the form a + bi, where a and b are real numbers called the real part and the imaginary part of the _____, respectively.

_____s are a field, and thus have addition, subtraction, multiplication, and division operations. These operations extend the corresponding operations on real numbers, although with a number of additional elegant and useful properties, e.g., negative real numbers can be obtained by squaring _____s.

a. 120-cell
b. Real part
c. 1-center problem
d. Complex number

35. In mathematics, the _____ is a geometric representation of the complex numbers established by the real axis and the orthogonal imaginary axis. It can be thought of as a modified Cartesian plane, with the real part of a complex number represented by a displacement along the x-axis, and the imaginary part by a displacement along the y-axis.

The _____ is sometimes called the Argand plane because it is used in Argand diagrams.

a. Complex plane
b. 120-cell
c. 1-center problem
d. 2-3 heap

36. In mathematics, an _____ is a complex number whose squared value is a real number less than or equal to zero. The imaginary unit, denoted by i or j, is an example of an _____. If y is a real number, then iÂ·y is an _____, because:

$$(i \cdot y)^2 = i^2 \cdot y^2 = -y^2 \leq 0.$$

They were defined in 1572 by Rafael Bombelli.

a. A Mathematical Theory of Communication
b. A chemical equation
c. Imaginary number
d. A posteriori

37. In mathematics, the _____ functions are functions of an angle; they are important when studying triangles and modeling periodic phenomena, among many other applications.
   a. Gudermannian function
   b. Coversine
   c. Law of sines
   d. Trigonometric

38. In algebra, a _____ of an element in a quadratic extension field of a field K is its image under the unique non-identity automorphism of the extended field that fixes K. If the extension is generated by a square root of an element r of K, then the _____ of $a + b\sqrt{r}$ is $a - b\sqrt{r}$ for $a, b \in K$, and in particular in the case of the field C of complex numbers as an extension of the field R of real numbers, the complex _____ of a + bi is a − bi.

Forming the sum or product of any element of the extension field with its _____ always gives an element of K.

a. Conjugate
b. Trinomial
c. Relation algebra
d. Real structure

39. In mathematics, a _____ is, informally, an infinitely vast and infinitely thin sheet. _____s may be thought of as objects in some higher dimensional space, or they may be considered without any outside space, as in the setting of Euclidean geometry
   a. Plane
   b. Group
   c. Bandwidth
   d. Blocking

40. In mathematics, the _____s may be described informally in several different ways. The _____s include both rational numbers, such as 42 and −23/129, and irrational numbers, such as pi and the square root of two; or, a _____ can be given by an infinite decimal representation, such as 2.4871773339...., where the digits continue in some way; or, the _____s may be thought of as points on an infinitely long number line.

These descriptions of the _____s, while intuitively accessible, are not sufficiently rigorous for the purposes of pure mathematics.

a. Real number
c. Minkowski distance
b. Pre-algebra
d. Tally marks

41. In mathematics, a _____ is the end result of a division problem. It can also be expressed as the number of times the divisor divides into the dividend.
  a. Marginal cost
  b. Limiting
  c. Notation
  d. Quotient

42. In simple terms, two events are _____ if they cannot occur at the same time.

In logic, two _____ propositions are propositions that logically cannot both be true. To say that more than two propositions are _____ may, depending on context mean that no two of them can both be true, or only that they cannot all be true.

  a. Determinism
  b. Mutually exclusive
  c. Philosophy
  d. Philosophy of mathematics

43. In vascular plants, the _____ is the organ of a plant body that typically lies below the surface of the soil. This is not always the case, however, since a _____ can also be aerial (that is, growing above the ground) or aerating (that is, growing up above the ground or especially above water.) Furthermore, a stem normally occurring below ground is not exceptional either
  a. 1-center problem
  b. 2-3 heap
  c. Root
  d. 120-cell

44. In probability theory, an _____ is a set of outcomes to which a probability is assigned. Typically, when the sample space is finite, any subset of the sample space is an _____. However, this approach does not work well in cases where the sample space is infinite, most notably when the outcome is a real number.
  a. Event
  b. Equaliser
  c. Information set
  d. Audio compression

45. A _____ of a number is a number a such that $a^3 = x$.
  a. Square root
  b. Cube root
  c. Hyperbolic functions
  d. Golden function

46. In mathematics, the nth _____ are all the complex numbers which yield 1 when raised to a given power n. It can be shown that they are located on the unit circle of the complex plane and that in that plane they form the vertices of an n-sided regular polygon with one vertex on 1.
  a. Square root of 2
  b. Roots of unity
  c. 120-cell
  d. 1-center problem

Chapter 9. Systems of Equations and Inequalities

1. _____ is an algebraic technique used to solve quadratic equations, in analytic geometry for determining the shapes of graphs, and in calculus for computing integrals. The essential objective is to reduce a quadratic polynomial in a variable in an equation or expression to a squared polynomial of linear order. This can reduce an equation or integral to one that is more easily solved or evaluated.

    a. Permanent of a matrix
    c. Monomial basis
    b. Relation algebra
    d. Completing the square

2. In linear algebra a matrix is in _____ if

    - All nonzero rows are above any rows of all zeroes, and
    - The leading coefficient of a row is always strictly to the right of the leading coefficient of the row above it.

This is the definition used in this article, but some texts add a third condition:

- The leading coefficient of each nonzero row is one.

A matrix is in reduced _____ if it satisfies the above three conditions, and if, in addition

- Every leading coefficient is the only nonzero entry in its column.

The first non-zero entry in each row is called a pivot.

This matrix is in reduced _____:

$$\begin{bmatrix} 0 & 1 & 4 & 0 & 0 \\ 0 & 0 & 0 & 1 & 0 \\ 0 & 0 & 0 & 0 & 1 \\ 0 & 0 & 0 & 0 & 0 \end{bmatrix}.$$

The following matrix is also in _____, but not in reduced row form:

$$\begin{bmatrix} 1 & 1 & 1 & 1 \\ 0 & 9 & 0 & 2 \\ 0 & 0 & 0 & 3 \end{bmatrix}.$$

However, this matrix is not in _____, as the leading coefficient of row 3 is not strictly to the right of the leading coefficient of row 2.

$$\begin{bmatrix} 1 & 2 & 3 & 4 \\ 0 & 3 & 7 & 2 \\ 0 & 2 & 0 & 0 \end{bmatrix}$$

Every non-zero matrix can be reduced to an infinite number of echelon forms via elementary matrix transformations.

a. Portable, Extensible Toolkit for Scientific Computation
b. Row echelon form
c. Reduced row echelon form
d. Gaussian elimination

3. In mathematics, a _____ is a rectangular table of elements, which may be numbers or, more generally, any abstract quantities that can be added and multiplied. Matrices are used to describe linear equations, keep track of the coefficients of linear transformations and to record data that depend on multiple parameters. Matrices are described by the field of _____ theory.

a. Matrix
b. Double counting
c. Coherent
d. Compression

4. In the study of metric spaces in mathematics, there are various notions of two metrics on the same underlying space being 'the same', or _____.

In the following, M will denote a non-empty set and d_1 and d_2 will denote two metrics on M.

The two metrics d_1 and d_2 are said to be topologically _____ if they generate the same topology on M.

a. A Mathematical Theory of Communication
b. A chemical equation
c. Equivalent
d. A posteriori

5. In quantum field theory and statistical mechanics in the thermodynamic limit, a system with a global symmetry can have more than one phase. For parameters where the symmetry is spontaneously broken, the system is said to be _____. When the global symmetry is unbroken the system is disordered.

a. Einstein relation
b. Isoenthalpic-isobaric ensemble
c. Ursell function
d. Ordered

6. A _____ is an algebraic equation in which each term is either a constant or the product of a constant and a single variable. _____s can have one, two, three or more variables.

_____s occur with great regularity in applied mathematics.

a. Quartic equation
b. Difference of two squares
c. Quadratic equation
d. Linear equation

7. In algebra, a _____ is a function depending on n that associates a scalar, de, to every n×n square matrix A. The fundamental geometric meaning of a _____ is as the scale factor for measure when A is regarded as a linear transformation. _____s are important both in calculus, where they enter the substitution rule for several variables, and in multilinear algebra.

Chapter 9. Systems of Equations and Inequalities

a. 1-center problem
c. Functional determinant
b. Determinant
d. Pfaffian

8. In logic, a theory is _____ if it does not contain a contradiction. The lack of contradiction can be defined in either semantic or syntactic terms. The semantic definition states that a theory is _____ if it has a model; this is the sense used in traditional Aristotelian logic, although in contemporary mathematical logic the term satisfiable is used instead.

a. Consistent
c. Logic
b. First-order logic
d. Second-order logic

9. In mathematics, an _____ is a statement about the relative size or order of two objects, or about whether they are the same or not

- The notation a < b means that a is less than b.
- The notation a > b means that a is greater than b.
- The notation a ≠ b means that a is not equal to b, but does not say that one is bigger than the other or even that they can be compared in size.

In all these cases, a is not equal to b, hence, '_____'.

These relations are known as strict _____

- The notation a ≤ b means that a is less than or equal to b;
- The notation a ≥ b means that a is greater than or equal to b;

An additional use of the notation is to show that one quantity is much greater than another, normally by several orders of magnitude.

- The notation a << b means that a is much less than b.
- The notation a >> b means that a is much greater than b.

If the sense of the _____ is the same for all values of the variables for which its members are defined, then the _____ is called an 'absolute' or 'unconditional' _____. If the sense of an _____ holds only for certain values of the variables involved, but is reversed or destroyed for other values of the variables, it is called a conditional _____.

An _____ may appear unsolvable because it only states whether a number is larger or smaller than another number; but it is possible to apply the same operations for equalities to inequalities. For example, to find x for the _____ 10x > 23 one would divide 23 by 10.

a. A Mathematical Theory of Communication
c. A posteriori
b. A chemical equation
d. Inequality

Chapter 9. Systems of Equations and Inequalities

10. _____ is the magnitude of change in the oscillating variable, with each oscillation, within an oscillating system. For instance, sound waves are oscillations in atmospheric pressure and their _____s are proportional to the change in pressure during one oscillation. If the variable undergoes regular oscillations, and a graph of the system is drawn with the oscillating variable as the vertical axis and time as the horizontal axis, the _____ is visually represented by the vertical distance between the extrema of the curve.

   a. Amplitude
   b. Angular frequency
   c. Angular velocity
   d. Areal velocity

11. In mathematics a _____ is an inequality which involves a linear function.

When operating in terms of real numbers, linear inequalities are the ones written in the forms

$$f(x) < b \text{ or } f(x) \leq b,$$

where f(x) is a linear functional in real numbers and b is a constant real number. Alternatively, these may be viewed as

$$g(x) < 0 \text{ or } g(x) \leq 0,$$

where g(x) is an affine function.

   a. Levi-Civita symbol
   b. Generalized singular value decomposition
   c. Split-complex number
   d. Linear inequality

12. _____ is either of the two parts into which a plane divides the three-dimensional space. More generally, a _____ is either of the two parts into which a hyperplane divides an affine space.

   a. Half-space
   b. Pendent
   c. Simple polytope
   d. Parallelogram law

13. In mathematics, the _____ of a real number is its numerical value without regard to its sign. So, for example, 3 is the _____ of both 3 and −3.

The _____ of a number a is denoted by $|a|$.

Generalizations of the _____ for real numbers occur in a wide variety of mathematical settings.

   a. Absolute value
   b. A Mathematical Theory of Communication
   c. A chemical equation
   d. Area hyperbolic functions

14. In mathematics, a _____ is a condition that a solution to an optimization problem must satisfy. There are two types of _____s: equality _____s and inequality _____s. The set of solutions that satisfy all _____s is called the feasible set.

   a. Decidable
   b. Constraint
   c. Foci
   d. Concurrent

Chapter 9. Systems of Equations and Inequalities

15. The mathematical concept of a _____ expresses the intuitive idea of deterministic dependence between two quantities, one of which is viewed as primary and the other as secondary. A _____ then is a way to associate a unique output for each input of a specified type, for example, a real number or an element of a given set.
   a. Function
   b. Coherent
   c. Going up
   d. Grill

16. In mathematics, _____ is a technique for optimization of a linear objective function, subject to linear equality and linear inequality constraints. Informally, _____ determines the way to achieve the best outcome in a given mathematical model given some list of requirements represented as linear equations.

More formally, given a polytope, and a real-valued affine function

$$f(x_1, x_2, \ldots, x_n) = c_1 x_1 + c_2 x_2 + \cdots + c_n x_n + d$$

defined on this polytope, a _____ method will find a point in the polytope where this function has the smallest value.

   a. Linear programming
   b. Descent direction
   c. Linear programming relaxation
   d. Lin-Kernighan

17. An _____ is a tree data structure in which each internal node has up to eight children. _____s are most often used to partition a three dimensional space by recursively subdividing it into eight octants. _____s are the three-dimensional analog of quadtrees.
   a. Interval tree
   b. External node
   c. Octree
   d. Adaptive k-d tree

18. The process of solving a linear system of equations that has been transformed into row-echelon form or reduced row-echelon form is _____. The last equation is solved first, then the next-to-last, and so.
   a. Jacobi rotation
   b. LU decomposition
   c. Crout matrix decomposition
   d. Back substitution

19. In linear algebra, the _____ of a matrix is obtained by changing a matrix in some way.

Given the matrices A and B, where:

$$A = \begin{bmatrix} 1 & 3 & 2 \\ 2 & 0 & 1 \\ 5 & 2 & 2 \end{bmatrix}, \quad B = \begin{bmatrix} 4 \\ 3 \\ 1 \end{bmatrix}$$

Then, the _____ is written as:

$$(A|B) = \begin{bmatrix} 1 & 3 & 2 & 4 \\ 2 & 0 & 1 & 3 \\ 5 & 2 & 2 & 1 \end{bmatrix}$$

This is useful when solving systems of linear equations or the _____ may also be used to find the inverse of a matrix by combining it with the identity matrix.

$$C = \begin{bmatrix} 1 & 3 \\ -5 & 0 \end{bmatrix}$$

Let C be a square 2×2 matrix where

To find the inverse of C we create where I is the 2×2 identity matrix.

a. Alternating sign matrix
b. Unimodular polynomial matrix
c. Eigendecomposition
d. Augmented matrix

20. In mathematics, a _____ is a constant multiplicative factor of a certain object. For example, in the expression $9x^2$, the _____ of x^2 is 9.

The object can be such things as a variable, a vector, a function, etc.

a. Fibonacci polynomials
b. Multivariate division algorithm
c. Stability radius
d. Coefficient

21. In mathematics, _____ is the operation of adding two matrices by adding the corresponding entries together. However, there is another operation which could also be considered as a kind of addition for matrices.

The usual _____ is defined for two matrices of the same dimensions.

a. Spectral theory
b. Jordan normal form
c. Standard basis
d. Matrix addition

22. In mathematics, an _____ or member of a set is any one of the distinct objects that make up that set.

Writing A = {1,2,3,4}, means that the _____s of the set A are the numbers 1, 2, 3 and 4. Groups of _____s of A, for example {1,2}, are subsets of A.

a. Element
b. Order
c. Ideal
d. Universal code

23. In mathematics, an _____ in the sense of ring theory is a subring $\mathcal{O}$ of a ring R that satisfies the conditions

1. R is a ring which is a finite-dimensional algebra over the rational number field $\mathbb{Q}$
2. $\mathcal{O}$ spans R over $\mathbb{Q}$, so that $\mathbb{Q}\mathcal{O} = R$, and
3. $\mathcal{O}$ is a lattice in R.

The third condition can be stated more accurately, in terms of the extension of scalars of R to the real numbers, embedding R in a real vector space. In less formal terms, additively $\mathcal{O}$ should be a free abelian group generated by a basis for R over $\mathbb{Q}$.

The leading example is the case where R is a number field K and $\mathcal{O}$ is its ring of integers. In algebraic number theory there are examples for any K other than the rational field of proper subrings of the ring of integers that are also _____s.

a. Annihilator
c. Efficiency
b. Order
d. Algebraic

24. In computational complexity theory, the complexity class _____ is the union of the classes in the exponential hierarchy.

$$\text{ELEMENTARY} = \text{EXP} \cup 2\text{EXP} \cup 3\text{EXP} \cup \cdots$$
$$= \text{DTIME}(2^n) \cup \text{DTIME}(2^{2^n}) \cup \text{DTIME}(2^{2^{2^n}}) \cup \cdots$$

The name was coined by Laszlo Kalmar, in the context of recursive functions and undecidability; most problems in it are far from _____. Some natural recursive problems lie outside _____, and are thus NONELEMENTARY.

a. A chemical equation
c. A posteriori
b. Elementary
d. A Mathematical Theory of Communication

25. _____ is a branch of mathematics which focuses on the study of matrices. Initially a sub-branch of linear algebra, it has grown to cover subjects related to graph theory, algebra, combinatorics, and statistics as well.

The term matrix was first coined in 1848 by J.J. Sylvester as a name of an array of numbers.

a. Pairing
c. Semi-simple operators
b. Segre classification
d. Matrix theory

26. In mathematics, the term _____ is frequently used for objects (for examples, groups or topological spaces) that have a very simple structure. For non-mathematicians, they are sometimes more difficult to visualize or understand than other, more complicated objects.

Examples include:

- empty set: the set containing no members
- _____ group: the mathematical group containing only the identity element
- _____ ring: a ring defined on a singleton set.

_____ also refers to solutions to an equation that have a very simple structure, but for the sake of completeness cannot be omitted. These solutions are called the _____ solution.

a. Per mil
c. Pure mathematics
b. Well-defined
d. Trivial

27. In mathematics, _____ are a concept central to linear algebra and related fields of mathematics

Suppose that K is a field and V is a vector space over K.

a. Setoid
c. Polarization
b. Linear combinations
d. Linear span

28. In combinatorial mathematics, a _____ is an un-ordered collection of distinct elements, usually of a prescribed size and taken from a given set. Given such a set S, a _____ of elements of S is just a subset of S, where as always forsets the order of the elements is not taken into account. Also, as always forsets, no elements can be repeated more than once in a _____; this is often referred to as a 'collection without repetition'.

a. Fill-in
c. Sparsity
b. Heawood number
d. Combination

29. In mathematics, the _____ of a number n is the number that, when added to n, yields zero. The _____ of n is denoted −n. For example, 7 is −7, because 7 + (−7) = 0, and the _____ of −0.3 is 0.3, because −0.3 + 0.3 = 0.

a. Arity
c. Algebraic structure
b. Additive inverse
d. Associativity

30. In mathematics, an arithmetic progression or _____ is a sequence of numbers such that the difference of any two successive members of the sequence is a constant. For instance, the sequence 3, 5, 7, 9, 11, 13... is an arithmetic progression with common difference 2.

a. Edgeworth series
c. Alternating series test
b. Eisenstein series
d. Arithmetic sequence

31. In mathematics, the _____s are an extension of the real numbers obtained by adjoining an imaginary unit, denoted i, which satisfies:

$$i^2 = -1.$$

Every _____ can be written in the form a + bi, where a and b are real numbers called the real part and the imaginary part of the _____, respectively.

_____s are a field, and thus have addition, subtraction, multiplication, and division operations. These operations extend the corresponding operations on real numbers, although with a number of additional elegant and useful properties, e.g., negative real numbers can be obtained by squaring _____s.

a. Complex number
b. Real part
c. 1-center problem
d. 120-cell

32. _____ is the mathematical operation of scaling one number by another. It is one of the four basic operations in elementary arithmetic.

_____ is defined for whole numbers in terms of repeated addition; for example, 4 multiplied by 3 can be calculated by adding 3 copies of 4 together:

$$4 + 4 + 4 = 12.$$

_____ of rational numbers and real numbers is defined by systematic generalization of this basic idea.

a. Least common multiple
b. The number 0 is even.
c. Highest common factor
d. Multiplication

33. In mathematics, the _____s may be described informally in several different ways. The _____s include both rational numbers, such as 42 and −23/129, and irrational numbers, such as pi and the square root of two; or, a _____ can be given by an infinite decimal representation, such as 2.4871773339...., where the digits continue in some way; or, the _____s may be thought of as points on an infinitely long number line.

These descriptions of the _____s, while intuitively accessible, are not sufficiently rigorous for the purposes of pure mathematics.

a. Pre-algebra
b. Tally marks
c. Real number
d. Minkowski distance

34. In linear algebra, a column vector or _____ is an m × 1 matrix, i.e. a matrix consisting of a single column of m elements.

$$\mathbf{x} = \begin{bmatrix} x_1 \\ x_2 \\ \vdots \\ x_m \end{bmatrix}$$

The transpose of a column vector is a row vector and vice versa.

The set of all column vectors forms a vector space which is the dual space to the set of all row vectors.

a. Spread of a matrix
b. Column matrix
c. Cayley-Hamilton theorem
d. Split-complex number

35. In linear algebra, a row vector or _____ is a 1 × n matrix, that is, a matrix consisting of a single row:

$$\mathbf{x} = \begin{bmatrix} x_1 & x_2 & \ldots & x_m \end{bmatrix}.$$

The transpose of a row vector is a column vector:

$$\begin{bmatrix} x_1 \\ x_2 \\ \vdots \\ x_m \end{bmatrix} = \begin{bmatrix} x_1 & x_2 & \ldots & x_m \end{bmatrix}^{\mathrm{T}}.$$

The set of all row vectors forms a vector space which is the dual space to the set of all column vectors.

Row vectors are sometimes written using the following non-standard notation:

$$\mathbf{x} = \begin{bmatrix} x_1, x_2, \ldots, x_m \end{bmatrix}.$$

- Matrix multiplication involves the action of multiplying each row vector of one matrix by each column vector of another matrix.

- The dot product of two vectors a and b is equivalent to multiplying the row vector representation of a by the column vector representation of b:

$$\mathbf{a} \cdot \mathbf{b} = \begin{bmatrix} a_1 & a_2 & a_3 \end{bmatrix} \begin{bmatrix} b_1 \\ b_2 \\ b_3 \end{bmatrix}.$$

a. Woodbury matrix identity
c. Dual vector space

b. Row matrix
d. Gram-Schmidt process

Chapter 9. Systems of Equations and Inequalities 93

36. In mathematics, the term _____ has several different important meanings:

- An _____ is an equality that remains true regardless of the values of any variables that appear within it, to distinguish it from an equality which is true under more particular conditions. For this, the 'triple bar' symbol ≡ is sometimes used.
- In algebra, an _____ or _____ element of a set S with a binary operation Â· is an element e that, when combined with any element x of S, produces that same x. That is, eÂ·x = xÂ·e = x for all x in S.
  - The _____ function from a set S to itself, often denoted id or id_S, s the function such that i = x for all x in S. This function serves as the _____ element in the set of all functions from S to itself with respect to function composition.
  - In linear algebra, the _____ matrix of size n is the n-by-n square matrix with ones on the main diagonal and zeros elsewhere. This matrix serves as the _____ with respect to matrix multiplication.

A common example of the first meaning is the trigonometric _____

$$\sin^2\theta + \cos^2\theta = 1$$

which is true for all real values of θ, as opposed to

$$\cos\theta = 1,$$

which is true only for some values of θ, not all. For example, the latter equation is true when $\theta = 0$, false when $\theta = 2$

The concepts of 'additive _____' and 'multiplicative _____' are central to the Peano axioms. The number 0 is the 'additive _____' for integers, real numbers, and complex numbers. For the real numbers, for all $a \in \mathbb{R}$,

$$0 + a = a,$$

$$a + 0 = a, \text{ and}$$

$$0 + 0 = 0.$$

Similarly, The number 1 is the 'multiplicative _____' for integers, real numbers, and complex numbers.

a. Identity
c. Action
b. ARIA
d. Intersection

37. In linear algebra, the _____ or unit matrix of size n is the n-by-n square matrix with ones on the main diagonal and zeros elsewhere. It is denoted by I_n, or simply by I if the size is immaterial or can be trivially determined by the context. (In some fields, such as quantum mechanics, the _____ is denoted by a boldface one, 1; otherwise it is identical to I.)

a. Unital
b. Arity
c. Associativity
d. Identity matrix

38. In linear algebra, a _____ of a matrix A is the determinant of some smaller square matrix, cut down from A by removing one or more of its rows or columns.

_____s obtained by removing just one row and one column from square matrices are required for calculating matrix cofactors, which in turn are useful for computing both the determinant and inverse of square matrices.

Let A be an m × n matrix and k an integer with 0 < k ≤ m, and k ≤ n.

a. Block size
b. Chiral
c. Homogeneity
d. Minor

39. In algebra, the _____ decomposition or _____ expansion is used to reduce the degree of either the numerator or the denominator of a rational function. The outcome of _____ expansion expresses that function as a sum of fractions, where:

- the denominator of each term is a power of an irreducible polynomial and
- the numerator is a polynomial of smaller degree than that irreducible polynomial.

See _____s in integration for an account of their use in finding antiderivatives. They are also used in calculating the inverse of transforms; such as the Laplace transform, or the Z-transform.

The basic idea behind _____s is to work backwards to separate a function.

a. Continuant
b. Concept algebra
c. Real structure
d. Partial fraction

Chapter 10. Sequences, Series, and Probability

1. The mathematical concept of a _____ expresses the intuitive idea of deterministic dependence between two quantities, one of which is viewed as primary and the other as secondary. A _____ then is a way to associate a unique output for each input of a specified type, for example, a real number or an element of a given set.
   a. Going up
   b. Grill
   c. Coherent
   d. Function

2. A more formal definition of a finite sequence with terms in a set S is a function from {1, 2, ..., n} to S for some n ≥ 0. An _____ in S is a function from {1, 2, ...} (the set of natural numbers without 0) to S.

Sequences may also start from 0, so the first term in the sequence is then a_0.

   a. A Mathematical Theory of Communication
   b. A chemical equation
   c. A posteriori
   d. Infinite sequence

3. In simple terms, two events are _____ if they cannot occur at the same time.

In logic, two _____ propositions are propositions that logically cannot both be true. To say that more than two propositions are _____ may, depending on context mean that no two of them can both be true, or only that they cannot all be true.

   a. Determinism
   b. Philosophy
   c. Philosophy of mathematics
   d. Mutually exclusive

4. In mathematics, the _____ of a real number is its numerical value without regard to its sign. So, for example, 3 is the _____ of both 3 and −3.

The _____ of a number a is denoted by $|a|$.

Generalizations of the _____ for real numbers occur in a wide variety of mathematical settings.

   a. A Mathematical Theory of Communication
   b. Absolute value
   c. A chemical equation
   d. Area hyperbolic functions

5. In probability theory, an _____ is a set of outcomes to which a probability is assigned. Typically, when the sample space is finite, any subset of the sample space is an _____. However, this approach does not work well in cases where the sample space is infinite, most notably when the outcome is a real number.
   a. Equaliser
   b. Information set
   c. Audio compression
   d. Event

6. In mathematics, a _____ is an expression constructed from variables and constants, using the operations of addition, subtraction, multiplication, and constant non-negative whole number exponents. For example, $x^2 - 4x + 7$ is a _____, but $x^2 - 4/x + 7x^{3/2}$ is not, because its second term involves division by the variable x and also because its third term contains an exponent that is not a whole number.

_____s are one of the most important concepts in algebra and throughout mathematics and science.

a. Coimage
c. Group extension
b. Semifield
d. Polynomial

7. _____ is the magnitude of change in the oscillating variable, with each oscillation, within an oscillating system. For instance, sound waves are oscillations in atmospheric pressure and their _____s are proportional to the change in pressure during one oscillation. If the variable undergoes regular oscillations, and a graph of the system is drawn with the oscillating variable as the vertical axis and time as the horizontal axis, the _____ is visually represented by the vertical distance between the extrema of the curve.
   a. Amplitude
   c. Angular velocity
   b. Areal velocity
   d. Angular frequency

8. A _____ or inductive definition is one that defines something in terms of itself, albeit in a useful way. For it to work, the definition in any given case must be well-founded, avoiding an infinite regress.

In simple terms, the _____ is one that grows an awareness and clarity upon itself toward a conclusive end, with each recurrence contributing something new toward the end definition.

   a. 1-center problem
   c. 120-cell
   b. 2-3 heap
   d. Recursive definition

9. _____ is the addition of a set of numbers; the result is their sum or total. An interim or present total of a _____ process is termed the running total. The 'numbers' to be summed may be natural numbers, complex numbers, matrices, or still more complicated objects.
   a. 1-center problem
   c. 2-3 heap
   b. 120-cell
   d. Summation

10. In mathematics, _____ and undefined are used to explain whether or not expressions have meaningful, sensible, and unambiguous values. Not all branches of mathematics come to the same conclusion.

The following expressions are undefined in all contexts, but remarks in the analysis section may apply.

   a. Defined
   c. Plugging in
   b. Toy model
   d. LHS

11. In mathematics, an algebraic group G contains a unique maximal normal solvable subgroup; and this subgroup is closed. Its identity component is called the _____ of G.
   a. Barycentric coordinates
   c. Block size
   b. Composite
   d. Radical

12. Call S_N the _____ to N of the sequence $\{a_n\}$, or _____ of the series. A series is the sequence of _____s, $\{S_N\}$.

When talking about series, one can refer either to the sequence $\{S_N\}$ of the _____s, or to the sum of the series,

$$\sum_{n=0}^{\infty} a_n$$

i.e., the limit of the sequence of _____s - it is clear which one is meant from context.

a. Binomial series
b. Calculus
c. Hyperbolic angle
d. Partial sum

13. In mathematics, an arithmetic progression or _____ is a sequence of numbers such that the difference of any two successive members of the sequence is a constant. For instance, the sequence 3, 5, 7, 9, 11, 13... is an arithmetic progression with common difference 2.
a. Edgeworth series
b. Eisenstein series
c. Arithmetic sequence
d. Alternating series test

14. In mathematics, a _____ is a statement that can be proved on the basis of explicitly stated or previously agreed assumptions.
a. Boolean function
b. Logical value
c. Disjunction introduction
d. Theorem

15. In mathematics and statistics, the _____ of a list of numbers is the sum of all of the list divided by the number of items in the list. If the list is a statistical population, then the mean of that population is called a population mean. If the list is a statistical sample, we call the resulting statistic a sample mean.
a. Interval estimation
b. Analysis of variance
c. Unsolved problems in statistics
d. Arithmetic mean

16. In mathematics, an _____, or central tendency of a data set refers to a measure of the 'middle' or 'expected' value of the data set. There are many different descriptive statistics that can be chosen as a measurement of the central tendency of the data items.

An _____ is a single value that is meant to typify a list of values.

a. A Mathematical Theory of Communication
b. Average
c. A posteriori
d. A chemical equation

17. In statistics, _____ has two related meanings:

- the arithmetic _____.
- the expected value of a random variable, which is also called the population _____.

Chapter 10. Sequences, Series, and Probability

It is sometimes stated that the '_____' _____s average. This is incorrect if '_____' is taken in the specific sense of 'arithmetic _____' as there are different types of averages: the _____, median, and mode. For instance, average house prices almost always use the median value for the average.

For a real-valued random variable X, the _____ is the expectation of X.

a. Statistical population
b. Proportional hazards model
c. Probability
d. Mean

18. The _____, in mathematics, is a type of mean or average, which indicates the central tendency or typical value of a set of numbers. It is similar to the arithmetic mean, which is what most people think of with the word 'average,' except that instead of adding the set of numbers and then dividing the sum by the count of numbers in the set, n, the numbers are multiplied and then the nth root of the resulting product is taken.

For instance, the _____ of two numbers, say 2 and 8, is just the square root (i.e., the second root) of their product, 16, which is 4.

a. Correlation
b. Skewness
c. Stratified sampling
d. Geometric mean

19. In mathematics, a _____ is a series with a constant ratio between successive terms. For example, the series

$$\frac{1}{2} + \frac{1}{4} + \frac{1}{8} + \frac{1}{16} + \cdots$$

is geometric, because each term is equal to half of the previous term. The sum of this series is 1, as illustrated in the following picture:

_____ are one of the simplest examples of infinite series with finite sums.

a. Riemann series theorem
b. Summation by parts
c. Telescoping series
d. Geometric series

20. In mathematics, a _____ is often represented as the sum of a sequence of terms. That is, a _____ is represented as a list of numbers with addition operations between them, for example this arithmetic sequence:

1 + 2 + 3 + 4 + 5 + ... + 99 + 100

In most cases of interest the terms of the sequence are produced according to a certain rule, such as by a formula, by an algorithm, by a sequence of measurements, or even by a random number generator.

a. Concavity
b. Contact
c. Series
d. Blind

Chapter 10. Sequences, Series, and Probability

21. The sum of an _____ $a_0 + a_1 + a_2 + â€¦$ is the limit of the sequence of partial sums

$$S_n = a_0 + a_1 + a_2 + \cdots + a_n,$$

as $n \to \infty$, if that limit exists. If the limit exists and is finite, the series is said to converge; if it is infinite or does not exist, the series is said to diverge.

The easiest way that an _____ can converge is if all the a_n are zero for n sufficiently large. Such a series can be identified with a finite sum, so it is only infinite in a trivial sense.

However, _____ of nonzero terms can also converge, which resolves the mathematical side of several of Zeno's paradoxes.

    a. Archimedes' use of infinitesimals   b. Uniform convergence
    c. Interpolation   d. Infinite series

22. In mathematics, a _____ is a number which can be expressed as a ratio of two integers. Non-integer _____s are usually written as the vulgar fraction $\frac{a}{b}$, where b is not zero. a is called the numerator, and b the denominator.
    a. Tally marks   b. Pre-algebra
    c. Minkowski distance   d. Rational number

23. _____ is a method of mathematical proof typically used to establish that a given statement is true of all natural numbers. It is done by proving that the first statement in the infinite sequence of statements is true, and then proving that if any one statement in the infinite sequence of statements is true, then so is the next one.

The method can be extended to prove statements about more general well-founded structures, such as trees; this generalization, known as structural induction, is used in mathematical logic and computer science.

    a. Herbrand structure   b. Mathematical induction
    c. Finitary   d. Ground expression

24. In elementary algebra, a _____ is a polynomial with two terms: the sum of two monomials. It is the simplest kind of polynomial except for a monomial.

The _____ $a^2 - b^2$ can be factored as the product of two other _____s:

    $a^2 - b^2$.

The product of a pair of linear _____s a x + b and c x + d is:

    2 +x + bd.

Chapter 10. Sequences, Series, and Probability

A _____ raised to the nth power, represented as

n

can be expanded by means of the _____ theorem or, equivalently, using Pascal's triangle.

a. Cylindrical algebraic decomposition
c. Real structure
b. Rational root theorem
d. Binomial

25. In mathematics, the _____ is an important formula giving the expansion of powers of sums. Its simplest version states that

$$(x+y)^n = \sum_{k=0}^{n} \binom{n}{k} x^{n-k} y^k \quad (1)$$

for any real or complex numbers x and y, and any nonnegative integer n. The binomial coefficient appearing in may be defined in terms of the factorial function n!:

$$\binom{n}{k} = \frac{n!}{k!(n-k)!}.$$

For example, here are the cases where $2 \leq n \leq 5$:

$$(x+y)^2 = x^2 + 2xy + y^2$$
$$(x+y)^3 = x^3 + 3x^2y + 3xy^2 + y^3$$
$$(x+y)^4 = x^4 + 4x^3y + 6x^2y^2 + 4xy^3 + y^4$$
$$(x+y)^5 = x^5 + 5x^4y + 10x^3y^2 + 10x^2y^3 + 5xy^4 + y^5.$$

Formula is valid more generally for any elements x and y of a semiring as long as xy = yx..

a. Stirling transform
c. Binomial theorem
b. Hypergeometric identities
d. Lah numbers

26. In mathematics, the _____ $\binom{n}{k}$ is the coefficient of the x^k term in the polynomial expansion of the binomial power ^{n}.

In combinatorics, $\binom{n}{k}$ is interpreted as the number of k-element subsets of an n-element set, that is the number of ways that k things can be 'chosen' from a set of n things. Hence, $\binom{n}{k}$ is often read as 'n choose k' and called the choose function of n and k.

a. Symbolic combinatorics
c. Binomial coefficient

b. Rule of product
d. Dyson conjecture

27. In mathematics, a _____ is a constant multiplicative factor of a certain object. For example, in the expression $9x^2$, the _____ of x^2 is 9.

The object can be such things as a variable, a vector, a function, etc.

a. Multivariate division algorithm
c. Fibonacci polynomials

b. Stability radius
d. Coefficient

28. In mathematics, the _____ of a non-negative integer n, denoted by n!, is the product of all positive integers less than or equal to n. For example,

$$5! = 1 \times 2 \times 3 \times 4 \times 5 = 120$$

and
$$6! = 1 \times 2 \times 3 \times 4 \times 5 \times 6 = 720$$

The notation n! was introduced by Christian Kramp in 1808.

The _____ function is formally defined by

$$n! = \prod_{k=1}^{n} k \qquad \forall n \in \mathbb{N}.$$

The above definition incorporates the instance

$$0! = 1$$

as an instance of the fact that the product of no numbers at all is 1.

a. Factorial
c. Symbolic combinatorics

b. Partition of a set
d. Plane partition

29. In mathematics, a _____ is the end result of a division problem. It can also be expressed as the number of times the divisor divides into the dividend.

a. Notation
c. Quotient

b. Marginal cost
d. Limiting

30. In mathematics, a _____ is a number that can be expressed as an integral of an algebraic function over an algebraic domain. Kontsevich and Zagier define a _____ as a complex number whose real and imaginary parts are values of absolutely convergent integrals of rational functions with rational coefficients, over domains in given by polynomial inequalities with rational coefficients.

   a. Closeness
   b. Disk
   c. Boussinesq approximation
   d. Period

31. A _____ is one of the basic shapes of geometry: a polygon with three corners or vertices and three sides or edges which are line segments. A _____ with vertices A, B, and C is denoted ABC.

   In Euclidean geometry any three non-collinear points determine a unique _____ and a unique plane.

   a. Triangle
   b. Fuhrmann circle
   c. 1-center problem
   d. Kepler triangle

32. In several fields of mathematics the term _____ is used with different but closely related meanings. They all relate to the notion of mapping the elements of a set to other elements of the same set, i.e., exchanging elements of a set.

   The general concept of _____ can be defined more formally in different contexts:

   In combinatorics, a _____ is usually understood to be a sequence containing each element from a finite set once, and only once.

   a. Linearly independent
   b. Permutation
   c. Tensor product
   d. Cyclic permutation

33. In set theory, a _____ is a partially ordered set such that for each t ∈ T, the set {s ∈ T : s < t} is well-ordered by the relation <. For each t ∈ T, the order type of {s ∈ T : s < t} is called the height of t. The height of T itself is the least ordinal greater than the height of each element of T.

   a. Definable numbers
   b. Set-theoretic topology
   c. Tree
   d. Transitive reduction

34. A _____ is a 2D geometric symbolic representation of information according to some visualization technique. Sometimes, the technique uses a 3D visualization which is then projected onto the 2D surface. The word graph is sometimes used as a synonym for _____.

   a. 120-cell
   b. 1-center problem
   c. 2-3 heap
   d. Diagram

35. In quantum field theory and statistical mechanics in the thermodynamic limit, a system with a global symmetry can have more than one phase. For parameters where the symmetry is spontaneously broken, the system is said to be _____. When the global symmetry is unbroken the system is disordered.

   a. Einstein relation
   b. Isoenthalpic-isobaric ensemble
   c. Ursell function
   d. Ordered

Chapter 10. Sequences, Series, and Probability

36. In combinatorial mathematics, a _____ is an un-ordered collection of distinct elements, usually of a prescribed size and taken from a given set. Given such a set S, a _____ of elements of S is just a subset of S, where as always forsets the order of the elements is not taken into account. Also, as always forsets, no elements can be repeated more than once in a _____; this is often referred to as a 'collection without repetition'.
  - a. Sparsity
  - b. Combination
  - c. Fill-in
  - d. Heawood number

37. In mathematics, especially in set theory, a set A is a _____ of a set B if A is 'contained' inside B. Notice that A and B may coincide. The relationship of one set being a _____ of another is called inclusion.
  - a. Cartesian product
  - b. Horizontal line test
  - c. Subset
  - d. Set of all sets

38. In scientific inquiry, an _____ is a method of investigating particular types of research questions or solving particular types of problems. The _____ is a cornerstone in the empirical approach to acquiring deeper knowledge about the world and is used in both natural sciences as well as in social sciences. An _____ is defined, in science, as a method of investigating less known fields, solving practical problems and proving theoretical assumptions.
  - a. A chemical equation
  - b. Experiment
  - c. A posteriori
  - d. A Mathematical Theory of Communication

39. In game theory, an _____ is a set of moves or strategies taken by the players, or their payoffs resulting from the actions or strategies taken by all players. The two are complementary in that given knowledge of the set of strategies of all players, the final state of the game is known, as are any relevant payoffs. In a game where chance or a random event is involved, the _____ is not known from only the set of strategies, but is only realized when the random even are realized.
  - a. Algebraic
  - b. Autonomous system
  - c. Equaliser
  - d. Outcome

40. _____ is the likelihood or chance that something is the case or will happen. Theoretical _____ is used extensively in areas such as statistics, mathematics, science and philosophy to draw conclusions about the likelihood of potential events and the underlying mechanics of complex systems.

  The word _____ does not have a consistent direct definition.

  - a. Statistical significance
  - b. Discrete random variable
  - c. Standardized moment
  - d. Probability

41. In statistics, a _____ is a subset of a population. Typically, the population is very large, making a census or a complete enumeration of all the values in the population impractical or impossible. The _____ represents a subset of manageable size.
  - a. Dispersion
  - b. Boussinesq approximation
  - c. Sample
  - d. Duality

42. In probability theory, the _____ or universal _____, often denoted S, Ω of an experiment or random trial is the set of all possible outcomes. For example, if the experiment is tossing a coin, the _____ is the set {head, tail}. For tossing a single six-sided die, the _____ is {1, 2, 3, 4, 5, 6}.

a. Martingale central limit theorem
c. Marginal distribution
b. Markov chain
d. Sample space

43. In discrete mathematics and predominantly in set theory, a _____ is a concept used in comparisons of sets to refer to the unique values of one set in relation to another. The terms 'absolute' and 'relative' _____ refer to more specific applications of the concept, with universal _____s referring to elements unique to the universal set and the latter referring to the unique elements of one set in relation to another. In this image, the universal set is represented by the border of the image, and the set A as a disc.
   a. Kernel
   c. Derivative algebra
   b. Huge
   d. Complement

44. In probability theory and statistics the _____ in favour of an event or a proposition are the quantity p /, where p is the probability of the event or proposition. The _____ against the same event are / p. For example, if you chose a random day of the week, then the _____ that you would choose a Sunday would be 1/6, not 1/7.
   a. Anscombe transform
   c. Odds
   b. Estimation of covariance matrices
   d. Event

45. In probability theory and statistics, the _____ of a random variable is the integral of the random variable with respect to its probability measure. For discrete random variables this is equivalent to the probability-weighted sum of the possible values, and for continuous random variables with a density function it is the probability density -weighted integral of the possible values.

The _____ may be intuitively understood by the law of large numbers: The _____, when it exists, is almost surely the limit of the sample mean as sample size grows to infinity.

   a. Expected value
   c. Illustration
   b. Event
   d. Infinitely divisible distribution

Chapter 11. Topics from Analytic Geometry

1. A _____ is a simple shape of Euclidean geometry consisting of those points in a plane which are at a constant distance, called the radius, from a fixed point, called the center. A _____ with center A is sometimes denoted by the symbol A.

A chord of a _____ is a line segment whose two endpoints lie on the _____.

   a. Circular segment
   b. Circumcircle
   c. Malfatti circles
   d. Circle

2. In mathematics, a _____ is a curve obtained by intersecting a cone with a plane. A _____ is therefore a restriction of a quadric surface to the plane. The _____s were named and studied as long ago as 200 BC, when Apollonius of Perga undertook a systematic study of their properties.
   a. Directrix
   b. Parabola
   c. Dandelin sphere
   d. Conic section

3. The latus rectum (2l) is the chord parallel to the _____ and passing through the focus (or one of the two foci.)

The semi-latus rectum (l) is half the latus rectum.

The focal parameter (p) is the distance from the focus (or one of the two foci) to the _____.

   a. Parabola
   b. Directrix
   c. Conic section
   d. Matrix representation of conic sections

4. In mathematics an _____ , a 'falling short') is a conic section, the locus of points in a plane such that the sum of the distances to two fixed points is equal to a given constant. The two fixed points are then called foci.

Another way is to define it as the path traced out by a point whose distance from a focus maintains a constant ratio less than one with its distance from a straight line not passing through the focus, called the directrix.

   a. A Mathematical Theory of Communication
   b. A posteriori
   c. Ellipse
   d. A chemical equation

5. In mathematics, the _____ is a conic section, the intersection of a right circular conical surface and a plane parallel to a generating straight line of that surface. Given a point and a line that lie in a plane, the locus of points in that plane that are equidistant to them is a _____.

A particular case arises when the plane is tangent to the conical surface of a circle.

   a. Directrix
   b. Dandelin sphere
   c. Parabola
   d. Matrix representation of conic sections

6. In mathematics, the _____ of a real number is its numerical value without regard to its sign. So, for example, 3 is the _____ of both 3 and −3.

The _____ of a number a is denoted by | a | .

Chapter 11. Topics from Analytic Geometry

Generalizations of the _____ for real numbers occur in a wide variety of mathematical settings.

a. A chemical equation
b. Area hyperbolic functions
c. A Mathematical Theory of Communication
d. Absolute value

7. In geometry, a _____ is a special kind of point, usually a corner of a polygon, polyhedron, or higher dimensional polytope. In the geometry of curves a _____ is a point of where the first derivative of curvature is zero. In graph theory, a _____ is the fundamental unit out of which graphs are formed

a. Duality
b. Crib
c. Vertex
d. Dini

8. In geometry and trigonometry, an _____ is the figure formed by two rays sharing a common endpoint, called the vertex of the _____. The magnitude of the _____ is the 'amount of rotation' that separates the two rays, and can be measured by considering the length of circular arc swept out when one ray is rotated about the vertex to coincide with the other. Where there is no possibility of confusion, the term '_____' is used interchangeably for both the geometric configuration itself and for its angular magnitude.

a. A posteriori
b. A chemical equation
c. A Mathematical Theory of Communication
d. Angle

9. In algebra, a _____ of an element in a quadratic extension field of a field K is its image under the unique non-identity automorphism of the extended field that fixes K. If the extension is generated by a square root of an element r of K, then the _____ of $a + b\sqrt{r}$ is $a - b\sqrt{r}$ for $a, b \in K$, and in particular in the case of the field C of complex numbers as an extension of the field R of real numbers, the complex _____ of a + bi is a − bi.

Forming the sum or product of any element of the extension field with its _____ always gives an element of K.

a. Trinomial
b. Relation algebra
c. Conjugate
d. Real structure

10. In mathematics, a _____ is a quadric surface of special kind. There are two kinds of _____s: elliptic and hyperbolic. The elliptic _____ is shaped like an oval cup and can have a maximum or minimum point.

a. Homoeoid
b. Paraboloid
c. Dupin cyclide
d. Spheroid

11. In trigonometry, the _____ is a function defined as tan x = $^{\sin x}/_{\cos x}$. The function is so-named because it can be defined as the length of a certain segment of a _____ (in the geometric sense) to the unit circle. In plane geometry, a line is _____ to a curve, at some point, if both line and curve pass through the point with the same direction.

a. Projective connection
b. Tangent
c. Hopf conjectures
d. Conformal geometry

12. In geometry, the _____ to a curve at a given point is the straight line that 'just touches' the curve at that point. As it passes through the point of tangency, the _____ is 'going in the same direction' as the curve, and in this sense it is the best straight-line approximation to the curve at that point. The same definition applies to space curves and curves in n-dimensional Euclidean space.

Chapter 11. Topics from Analytic Geometry

a. Chern-Weil theory
b. Darboux frame
c. Four-vertex theorem
d. Tangent line

13. The term _____ or centre is used in various contexts in abstract algebra to denote the set of all those elements that commute with all other elements. More specifically:

- The _____ of a group G consists of all those elements x in G such that xg = gx for all g in G. This is a normal subgroup of G.
- The _____ of a ring R is the subset of R consisting of all those elements x of R such that xr = rx for all r in R. The _____ is a commutative subring of R, so R is an algebra over its _____.
- The _____ of an algebra A consists of all those elements x of A such that xa = ax for all a in A. See also: central simple algebra.
- The _____ of a Lie algebra L consists of all those elements x in L such that [x,a] = 0 for all a in L. This is an ideal of the Lie algebra L.
- The _____ of a monoidal category C consists of pairs *a natural isomorphism satisfying certain axioms*.

a. Disk
b. Block size
c. Brute Force
d. Center

14. In geometry, the _____ are a pair of special points used in describing conic sections. The four types of conic sections are the circle, parabola, ellipse, and hyperbola.
a. Heap
b. C-35
c. Boussinesq approximation
d. Foci

15. In geometry, the semi-_____ (also semimajor axis) is used to describe the dimensions of ellipses and hyperbolae.

The _____ of an ellipse is its longest diameter, a line that runs through the centre and both foci, its ends being at the widest points of the shape. The semi-_____ is one half of the _____, and thus runs from the centre, through a focus, and to the edge of the ellipse.

a. Semi-major axis
b. Major axis
c. Lagrange points
d. Lagrangian points

16. In linear algebra, a _____ of a matrix A is the determinant of some smaller square matrix, cut down from A by removing one or more of its rows or columns.

_____s obtained by removing just one row and one column from square matrices are required for calculating matrix cofactors, which in turn are useful for computing both the determinant and inverse of square matrices.

Let A be an m × n matrix and k an integer with 0 < k ≤ m, and k ≤ n.

a. Homogeneity
b. Chiral
c. Block size
d. Minor

17. In mathematics, the _____ of a Euclidean space is a special point, usually denoted by the letter O, used as a fixed point of reference for the geometry of the surrounding space. In a Cartesian coordinate system, the _____ is the point where the axes of the system intersect. In Euclidean geometry, the _____ may be chosen freely as any convenient point of reference.

a. Interval
b. OMAC
c. Autonomous system
d. Origin

18. An _____ is a type of quadric surface that is a higher dimensional analogue of an ellipse. The equation of a standard _____ body in an xyz-Cartesian coordinate system is

$$\frac{x^2}{a^2} + \frac{y^2}{b^2} + \frac{z^2}{c^2} = 1$$

where a and b are the equatorial radii and c is the polar radius, all of which are fixed positive real numbers determining the shape of the _____.

If all three radii are equal, the solid body is a sphere; if two radii are equal, the _____ is a spheroid:

- $a = b = c$: Sphere;
- c:,!" src="http://upload.wikimedia.org/math/1/c/1/1c101f69cb5c9fca2549cc52aa371d02.png"> Oblate spheroid;
- $a = b < c$: Prolate spheroid;
- b>c:,!" src="http://upload.wikimedia.org/math/f/f/4/ff41a00b219ea3edb0d41dce4d26cc46.png"> Scalene _____.

The points, and lie on the surface and the line segments from the origin to these points are called the semi-principal axes. These correspond to the semi-major axis and semi-minor axis of the appropriate ellipses.

a. A Mathematical Theory of Communication
b. A posteriori
c. A chemical equation
d. Ellipsoid

19. An _____ of a real-valued function y = f(x) is a curve which describes the behavior of f as either x or y tends to infinity.

In other words, as one moves along the graph of f(x) in some direction, the distance between it and the _____ eventually becomes smaller than any distance that one may specify.

If a curve A has the curve B as an _____, one says that A is asymptotic to B. Similarly B is asymptotic to A, so A and B are called asymptotic.

a. Improper integral
b. Isoperimetric dimension
c. Asymptote
d. Infinite product

20. In geometry, a _____ is defined as a quadrilateral where all four of its angles are right angles.
 a. Point group in two dimensions
 b. Polytope
 c. Cantor-Dedekind axiom
 d. Rectangle

21. A branch or tree branch (sometimes referred to in botany as a ramus) is a woody structural member connected to but not part of the central trunk of a tree (or sometimes a shrub.) Large _____ are known as boughs and small _____ are known as twigs.

While _____ can be nearly horizontal, vertical, or diagonal, the majority of trees have upwardly diagonal _____.

 a. 120-cell
 b. 2-3 heap
 c. 1-center problem
 d. Branches

22. In mathematics, the concept of a _____ tries to capture the intuitive idea of a geometrical one-dimensional and continuous object. A simple example is the circle. In everyday use of the term '_____', a straight line is not curved, but in mathematical parlance _____s include straight lines and line segments.
 a. Kappa curve
 b. Negative pedal curve
 c. Curve
 d. Quadrifolium

23. In mathematics, _____ are a method of defining a curve. A simple kinematical example is when one uses a time parameter to determine the position, velocity, and other information about a body in motion.

Abstractly, a relation is given in the form of an equation, and it is shown also to be the image of functions from items such as R^n.

 a. Multipole moment
 b. Laplace operator
 c. Differential operator
 d. Parametric equations

24. In mathematics, a _____ is, informally, an infinitely vast and infinitely thin sheet. _____s may be thought of as objects in some higher dimensional space, or they may be considered without any outside space, as in the setting of Euclidean geometry
 a. Bandwidth
 b. Group
 c. Blocking
 d. Plane

25. In mathematics, a _____ is a curve in a Euclidian plane. The most frequently studied cases are smooth _____s, and algebraic _____s.

A smooth _____ is a curve in a real Euclidian plane R^2 is a one-dimensional smooth manifold.

Chapter 11. Topics from Analytic Geometry

a. General position
b. Corresponding sides
c. Subtended
d. Plane curve

26. In abstract algebra, a module S over a ring R is called _____ or irreducible if it is not the zero module 0 and if its only submodules are 0 and S. Understanding the _____ modules over a ring is usually helpful because these modules form the 'building blocks' of all other modules in a certain sense.

Abelian groups are the same as Z-modules.

a. Derivation
b. Simple
c. Basis
d. Harmonic series

27. _____ is the magnitude of change in the oscillating variable, with each oscillation, within an oscillating system. For instance, sound waves are oscillations in atmospheric pressure and their _____s are proportional to the change in pressure during one oscillation. If the variable undergoes regular oscillations, and a graph of the system is drawn with the oscillating variable as the vertical axis and time as the horizontal axis, the _____ is visually represented by the vertical distance between the extrema of the curve.

a. Angular frequency
b. Areal velocity
c. Angular velocity
d. Amplitude

28. _____ are a three-dimensional orthogonal coordinate system that results from rotating the two-dimensional elliptic coordinate system about the focal axis of the ellipse. Rotation about the other axis produces the oblate spheroidal coordinates.

This coordinate system can be used to solve various partial differential equations in which the boundary conditions match its symmetry and shape, such as solving for a field produced by two centers, which are taken as the foci on the z-axis.

a. 2-3 heap
b. 1-center problem
c. 120-cell
d. Prolate spheroidal coordinates

29. In mathematics, a _____ is a planar simple closed curve such that when traveling on it one always has the curve interior to the left. If in the above definition one interchanges left and right, one obtains a negatively oriented curve.

Crucial to this definition is the fact that every simple closed curve admits a well-defined interior; that follows from the Jordan curve theorem.

a. Lemniscate of Bernoulli
b. Whewell equation
c. Positively oriented curve
d. Sinusoidal spiral

30. In graph theory, a _____ in a graph is a sequence of vertices such that from each of its vertices there is an edge to the next vertex in the sequence. The first vertex is called the start vertex and the last vertex is called the end vertex. Both of them are called end or terminal vertices of the _____.

a. Path
b. Deltoid
c. Blinding
d. Class

31. A _____ is the curve defined by the path of a point on the edge of circular wheel as the wheel rolls along a straight line. It is an example of a roulette, a curve generated by a curve rolling on another curve.

The _____ is the solution to the brachistochrone problem and the related tautochrone problem.

a. Hessian curve
c. Superformula

b. Hippopede
d. Cycloid

32. In singularity theory a _____ is a singular point of a curve. Spinode is an alternative name, but this is less commonly used today.

For a curve defined as the zero set of a function of two variables f, the _____ s on the curve will have the following properties:

1. $f(x, y) = 0$
2. $\dfrac{\partial f}{\partial x} = \dfrac{\partial f}{\partial y} = 0$
3. The Hessian matrix of second derivatives has zero determinant.

A classic example of a curve that exhibits a _____ is the curve defined by

$$x^3 - y^2 = 0$$

This curve can be expressed parametrically by the equations

$$x = t^2, y = t^3.$$

This curve has a _____ at the origin.

a. Character
c. Dense

b. Cusp
d. Brute Force

33. In mathematics, the idea of _____ has come to stand for a very general idea, extending the intuitive idea of 'gluing' in topology. Since the topologists' glue is actually the use of equivalence relations on topological spaces, the theory starts with some ideas on identification.

A sophisticated theory resulted.

a. Deviance
c. Block size

b. Dominance
d. Descent

Chapter 11. Topics from Analytic Geometry

34. In mathematics, the _____ system is a two-dimensional coordinate system in which each point on a plane is determined by an angle and a distance. The _____ system is especially useful in situations where the relationship between two points is most easily expressed in terms of angles and distance; in the more familiar Cartesian or rectangular coordinate system, such a relationship can only be found through trigonometric formulation.

As the coordinate system is two-dimensional, each point is determined by two _____s: the radial coordinate and the angular coordinate.

a. Sir Isaac Newton
b. Sequence alignment
c. Polar coordinate
d. Vampire

35. In complex analysis, a _____ of a meromorphic function is a certain type of singularity that behaves like the singularity $1/z^n$ at z = 0. This means that, in particular, a _____ of the function f

Formally, suppose U is an open subset of the complex plane C, a is an element of U and f : U − {a} → C is a function which is holomorphic over its domain.

a. Pole
b. Dini
c. Harmonic series
d. Decidable

36. In mathematics, the _____ is a two-dimensional coordinate system in which each point on a plane is determined by an angle and a distance. The _____ is especially useful in situations where the relationship between two points is most easily expressed in terms of angles and distance; in the more familiar Cartesian or rectangular coordinate system, such a relationship can only be found through trigonometric formulation.

As the coordinate system is two-dimensional, each point is determined by two polar coordinates: the radial coordinate and the angular coordinate.

a. Sir Isaac Newton
b. Marian Adam Rejewski
c. ROT13
d. Polar coordinate system

37. In mathematics, a _____ is the end result of a division problem. It can also be expressed as the number of times the divisor divides into the dividend.
a. Quotient
b. Limiting
c. Marginal cost
d. Notation

38. _____ is closed curve with one cusp.

Chapter 11. Topics from Analytic Geometry

In geometry, the _____ is an epicycloid with one cusp.

Rolling circle around another fixed circle produces _____ Conformal mapping from circle to _____

- epicycloid produced as the path of a point on the circumference of a circle as that circle rolls around another fixed circle with the same radius.

- limaçon with one cusp. The cusp is formed when the ratio of a to b in the equation is equal to one.

a. 2-3 heap
c. 1-center problem
b. 120-cell
d. Cardioid

39. In mathematics, a real-valued function f defined on an interval is called _____, concave upwards, concave up or _____ cup, if for any two points x and y in its domain C and any t in [0,1], we have

$$f(tx + (1-t)y) \leq tf(x) + (1-t)f(y).$$

_____ function on an interval.

In other words, a function is _____ if and only if its epigraph is a _____ set.

Pictorially, a function is called '_____' if the function lies below the straight line segment connecting two points, for any two points in the interval.

A function is called strictly _____ if

$$f(tx + (1-t)y) < tf(x) + (1-t)f(y)$$

for any t in and $x \neq y$.

A function f is said to be concave if − f is _____.

a. Convex
c. Continuum
b. Contrapositive
d. Continuous wavelet

40. In mathematics, a _____ is a curve which emanates from a central point, getting progressively farther away as it revolves around the point. An Archimedean _____, a helix, and a conic _____.

A '_____' and a 'helix' are two terms that are easily confused, but represent different objects.

A _____ is typically a planar curve, like the groove on a record or the arms of a _____ galaxy.

a. Logarithmic spiral
b. Spiral
c. Fresnel integrals
d. Cornu spiral

41. In mathematics, a _____ or rhodonea curve is a sinusoid plotted in polar coordinates. Up to similarity, these curves can all be expressed by a polar equation of the form

$$r = \cos(k\theta).$$

If k is an integer, the curve will be _____ shaped with

- 2k petals if k is even, and
- k petals if k is odd.

When k is even, the entire graph of the _____ will be traced out exactly once when the value of θ changes from 0 to 2π. When k is odd, this will happen on the interval between 0 and π.

If k is rational, then the curve is closed and has finite length.

a. Sextic plane curve
b. Cycloid
c. Conchoid
d. Rose

42. In mathematics, a _____ is a statement that can be proved on the basis of explicitly stated or previously agreed assumptions.
a. Logical value
b. Boolean function
c. Disjunction introduction
d. Theorem

43. In mathematics, a _____ is a number that can be expressed as an integral of an algebraic function over an algebraic domain. Kontsevich and Zagier define a _____ as a complex number whose real and imaginary parts are values of absolutely convergent integrals of rational functions with rational coefficients, over domains in given by polynomial inequalities with rational coefficients.
a. Boussinesq approximation
b. Disk
c. Closeness
d. Period

44. In algebra, a _____ is a function depending on n that associates a scalar, de, to every n×n square matrix A. The fundamental geometric meaning of a _____ is as the scale factor for measure when A is regarded as a linear transformation. _____s are important both in calculus, where they enter the substitution rule for several variables, and in multilinear algebra.
a. Functional determinant
b. Determinant
c. 1-center problem
d. Pfaffian

45. In mathematics, the _____ of a number n is the number that, when added to n, yields zero. The _____ of n is denoted −n. For example, 7 is −7, because 7 + (−7) = 0, and the _____ of −0.3 is 0.3, because −0.3 + 0.3 = 0.
a. Arity
b. Algebraic structure
c. Associativity
d. Additive inverse

46. In mathematics, the _____ or cyclometric functions are the so-called inverse functions of the trigonometric functions, though they do not meet the official definition for inverse functions as their domains are subsets of the images of the original functions.
   a. A chemical equation
   b. A posteriori
   c. A Mathematical Theory of Communication
   d. Inverse trigonometric functions

47. In mathematics, the _____ functions are functions of an angle; they are important when studying triangles and modeling periodic phenomena, among many other applications.
   a. Gudermannian function
   b. Trigonometric
   c. Coversine
   d. Law of sines

48. In mathematics, the _____ are functions of an angle. They are important in the study of triangles and modeling periodic phenomena, among many other applications. _____ are commonly defined as ratios of two sides of a right triangle containing the angle, and can equivalently be defined as the lengths of various line segments from a unit circle.
   a. Trigonometric integrals
   b. Law of sines
   c. Trigonometric functions
   d. Sine

49. The mathematical concept of a _____ expresses the intuitive idea of deterministic dependence between two quantities, one of which is viewed as primary and the other as secondary. A _____ then is a way to associate a unique output for each input of a specified type, for example, a real number or an element of a given set.
   a. Grill
   b. Going up
   c. Function
   d. Coherent

Chapter 1

1. a	2. d	3. a	4. b	5. c	6. d	7. c	8. c	9. a	10. c
11. b	12. d	13. d	14. a	15. c	16. c	17. b	18. d	19. c	20. d
21. b	22. b	23. d	24. b	25. d	26. d	27. c	28. c	29. c	30. d
31. a	32. d	33. d	34. c	35. d	36. c	37. d	38. d	39. b	40. d
41. d	42. b	43. a	44. d	45. a	46. d	47. d	48. d	49. d	50. a
51. d	52. d	53. c	54. c	55. d	56. d	57. d			

Chapter 2

1. b	2. d	3. a	4. d	5. b	6. a	7. d	8. c	9. b	10. d
11. c	12. d	13. d	14. d	15. d	16. d	17. a	18. d	19. d	20. d
21. d	22. a	23. d	24. d	25. d	26. d	27. b	28. a	29. a	30. d
31. d	32. d	33. b	34. a	35. c	36. d	37. d	38. d	39. c	40. d
41. c	42. c	43. d	44. d						

Chapter 3

1. d	2. d	3. a	4. d	5. d	6. c	7. a	8. b	9. d	10. b
11. d	12. d	13. d	14. a	15. c	16. d	17. b	18. d	19. d	20. d
21. d	22. d	23. d	24. d	25. b	26. d	27. a	28. d	29. c	30. d
31. d	32. d	33. a	34. d	35. c	36. d	37. d	38. d	39. d	40. d
41. d	42. d	43. c	44. d	45. d	46. d	47. d	48. d	49. d	50. a
51. d	52. a	53. d	54. d	55. d	56. b	57. d	58. d	59. d	60. d
61. a	62. d	63. d	64. c	65. b	66. a	67. d	68. d	69. d	

Chapter 4

1. d	2. a	3. d	4. d	5. d	6. c	7. c	8. d	9. c	10. a
11. c	12. c	13. d	14. c	15. d	16. a	17. d	18. d	19. b	20. a
21. d	22. b	23. d	24. c	25. b	26. d	27. d	28. b	29. d	30. d
31. d	32. b								

Chapter 5

1. d	2. c	3. b	4. d	5. d	6. d	7. a	8. c	9. d	10. d
11. d	12. a	13. b	14. d	15. d	16. a	17. d	18. d	19. b	20. c
21. a	22. a	23. b	24. a	25. a	26. b	27. b	28. c	29. a	30. d
31. a	32. d	33. b	34. d	35. a	36. d	37. a	38. c	39. a	40. d
41. d									

Chapter 6

1. d	2. b	3. b	4. a	5. b	6. c	7. c	8. c	9. a	10. d
11. a	12. a	13. d	14. d	15. b	16. d	17. d	18. c	19. d	20. b
21. d	22. a	23. d	24. d	25. d	26. a	27. d	28. a	29. d	30. c
31. a	32. d	33. d	34. b	35. b	36. a	37. c	38. b	39. d	40. a
41. c	42. d	43. c	44. c	45. b	46. b	47. c	48. d	49. d	50. d
51. c	52. d	53. b	54. d	55. a	56. d	57. b	58. d	59. d	60. a
61. a	62. d	63. b	64. d	65. d					

ANSWER KEY

Chapter 7
1. d	2. a	3. d	4. a	5. d	6. c	7. d	8. d	9. c	10. b
11. c	12. d	13. d	14. d	15. d	16. d	17. d	18. b	19. b	20. d
21. d	22. d	23. d	24. d	25. d	26. d	27. d	28. a		

Chapter 8
1. a	2. d	3. c	4. a	5. a	6. d	7. a	8. d	9. c	10. d
11. d	12. d	13. c	14. b	15. d	16. a	17. d	18. a	19. d	20. d
21. d	22. d	23. c	24. b	25. b	26. b	27. b	28. d	29. b	30. a
31. d	32. d	33. d	34. d	35. a	36. c	37. d	38. a	39. a	40. a
41. d	42. b	43. c	44. a	45. b	46. b				

Chapter 9
1. d	2. b	3. a	4. c	5. d	6. d	7. b	8. a	9. d	10. a
11. d	12. a	13. a	14. b	15. a	16. a	17. c	18. d	19. d	20. d
21. d	22. a	23. b	24. b	25. d	26. d	27. b	28. d	29. b	30. d
31. a	32. d	33. c	34. b	35. b	36. a	37. d	38. d	39. d	

Chapter 10
1. d	2. d	3. d	4. b	5. d	6. d	7. a	8. d	9. d	10. a
11. d	12. d	13. c	14. d	15. d	16. b	17. d	18. d	19. d	20. c
21. d	22. d	23. b	24. d	25. c	26. c	27. d	28. a	29. c	30. d
31. a	32. b	33. c	34. d	35. d	36. b	37. c	38. b	39. d	40. d
41. c	42. d	43. d	44. c	45. a					

Chapter 11
1. d	2. d	3. b	4. c	5. c	6. d	7. c	8. d	9. c	10. b
11. b	12. d	13. d	14. d	15. b	16. d	17. d	18. d	19. c	20. d
21. d	22. c	23. d	24. d	25. d	26. b	27. d	28. d	29. c	30. a
31. d	32. b	33. d	34. c	35. a	36. d	37. a	38. d	39. a	40. b
41. d	42. d	43. d	44. b	45. d	46. d	47. b	48. c	49. c	